HARDANGER
EMBROIDERY

HARDANGER EMBROIDERY

20 Stunning Counted Thread Projects

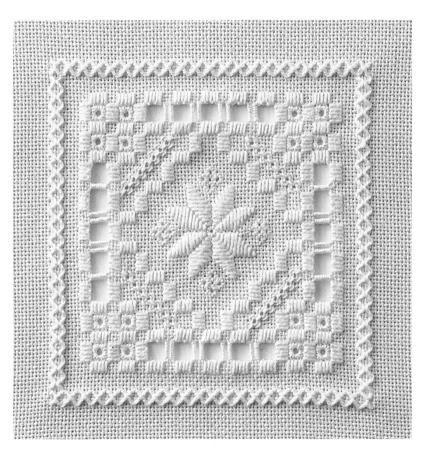

JILL CARTER

Quilters' Resource publications

DEDICATION

For my dear Norwegian friends, Agnes and Ivar Amundsen.

First published in 2000 by
Quilters' Resource Inc.
P.O. Box 148850
Chicago, IL 60614
Phone #773 278-5695
Email info@quiltersresource.com

ISBN 1-889682-14-4

Printed in China

Photography by Janine Hosegood
Sampler and cushions photographed by Michael Wicks
Illustrations by Siriol Clarry

Contents

INTRODUCTION

Along with skiing I was introduced to Hardanger embroidery thirty years ago when I lived in Oslo. My Norwegian teacher had been doing Hardanger all her life and taught us – a small group of Army wives who had never seen Hardanger before – with consummate skill and boundless enthusiasm. She not only taught us the techniques but insisted on an extremely high standard of workmanship, and she instilled in us the same love and appreciation for this disciplined and beautiful traditional Norwegian embroidery that she possessed.

If you can count, you can do Hardanger. This book is for all embroiderers who want to stitch. It will inspire those who may never have attempted or even seen Hardanger before; it will encourage those who know a little and would like to know more; it will intrigue those who know a lot but find there are some new stitches and ideas worth undertaking; and it will interest those who want to do the projects for the sheer enjoyment of making something in traditional Hardanger embroidery stitches while using modern threads and fabrics.

For the beginner, Hardanger is not as alarming as it might appear. By following the very comprehensive section on materials, techniques and stitches, the novice will discover all that is necessary to make a start and develop a good technical grounding in Hardanger. In addition, there are some appealing but uncomplicated filling stitches and edgings to try out. More advanced stitchers will find some surprises, as I have introduced interesting ideas for incorporating beads as part of fillings or edgings.

Work the projects that appeal to you and do not choose them just because you think they look easy. I have designed the projects so that there is nothing that a beginner could not tackle, and they can all be made more simple or developed further to interpret your own ideas. The projects themselves, which are divided into three themed sections, are a mixture of the contemporary and the traditional but have a relevance to our lives today.

I have used colour with circumspection and only where it is appropriate. Beads and metallic threads offer another dimension and proved to be irresistible, but essentially the magic of Hardanger embroidery is white on white.

HISTORY OF HARDANGER EMBROIDERY

Hardanger embroidery takes its name from the Hardanger region of southwest Norway in the county of Hordaland. Along with many other types of folk embroidery, the exact origins of this beautiful white work technique have been lost in the mists of time, but they are thought to emanate from the Middle East. Early forms of the technique spread to Europe to give Hardanger embroidery roots in the Reticella and Venetian needle-made 'lace' of Renaissance Italy, fashionably decorating coifs, shirts, ruffs, cuffs and linen textiles of that period. Hardanger has the distinct geometric character that is Reticella, which was based on a foundation of threads in squares, diagonals, triangles and arcs.

The Norwegians of the Hardanger region and west coast of Norway were adventurous traders and seafarers, travelling to eastern Europe and the Middle East and returning home with knowledge and skills acquired during the course of their long trading journeys. Slowly, from these intrepid beginnings, cut and drawn work became established in Norway and evolved into Hardanger embroidery as we now know it. In its earliest stages Hardanger designs were simple and worked with fine linen thread on 50-count linen. Squares were cut out and the resulting openings filled with an open network of threads. The åttebladsrose (literally translated as eight-petalled rose and also known as satin stitch star) found in so many other traditional folk embroidery throughout the world was also an early and important recurring motif in Hardanger embroidery.

From the seventeenth century, with the growth of flax that was carded and spun into thread and fabric, Hardanger became established and popular as an embroidery technique for decorating household linens, ecclesiastical pieces (there are wonderful examples from Hove and Hoprekstad churches), clothing and aprons worn with traditional folk costume (bunad) on festive and family occasions.

In this century there has been an important ground swell of awareness and interest in folk dress generally. Norwegians are proud of their rich inheritance and are

keen to uphold and perpetuate their traditions and embroidery skills. The costumes from the Hardanger regions are no exception. For example, the exquisitely worked embroidery in the old traditional Hardanger blouse in my collection shown opposite is stitched on a 44-count cotton with very fine thread. Hardanger designs are passed down or re-created and the results can be seen and admired on the aprons, collars, cuffs, front flaps of blouses and household items. The photograph of the traditional Hardanger marriage bunad worn by Ågot Gammersvik for her wedding shows you how that rich tradition still proudly survives.

CHAPTER 1

MATERIALS AND TECHNIQUES

ALL THE BASIC INSTRUCTIONS AND STEP-BY-STEP STITCH

ILLUSTRATIONS FOR HARDANGER ARE INCLUDED IN THIS

SECTION OF THE BOOK. IT WILL HELP IF YOU FAMILIARIZE

YOURSELF WITH THIS INFORMATION BEFORE YOU START

WORK ON ANY OF THE PROJECTS.

MATERIALS

Fabric

Hardanger embroidery is worked on any evenweave fabric of which the threads may be cut and withdrawn. You will be spending valuable time creating a beautiful and delicate piece of work, so always buy a good quality fabric so that the embroidery is shown to its best advantage.

There are many evenweave fabrics available to use for Hardanger, each one with different properties, not only in the make-up of the fabric but also in the thickness of the weave. Fabric weight is generally gauged by the number of threads to the inch, referred to as the 'count', or holes per the inch (HPI). It is important to understand the count of a fabric because it will determine the size of your stitches and the delicacy of the work. The higher the count (i.e. the number of threads to the inch) the finer the weave of the fabric and therefore the more elegant your Hardanger embroidery. That is not to say that it is any less attractive for being worked on a lower count fabric, merely more dense.

I prefer to work on an evenweave linen, such as Fabric Flair's Minster 100% linen 28 threads to the inch, because I love the texture and results of needleweaving and fillings on linen. I have found this linen easy to handle and use. It is possible to pull the needlewoven bars tightly and to make them look very fine and delicate. If you have difficulty keeping the threads straight as you needleweave, a very small amount of spray starch on the back of the work

will help to stablilize the grid and keep it in position. Linen may be found in various other counts, such as 21, 26, 32 and 35 threads to the inch, and Zweigart's Dublin 100% linen, 25 threads to the inch makes a good larger alternative. Permin linens in 28- and 32-count come in many colours and some are dyed to match Coton Perlé threads. Working on a 32-count fabric will result in beautifully fine needleweaving and exquisite fillings, but also requires good eyesight or, alternatively, an excellent magnifying glass.

I have used other cotton/mix evenweave fabrics, throughout the book, which I think particularly lend themselves to Hardanger embroidery either because of the colour or the way the fabric handles. Jobelan (52% cotton/48% viscose, 28 threads to the inch) and Zweigart's Lugana or Brittney (52% cotton and 48% rayon, 25 and 28 threads to the inch respectively) are very easy to work on. Kloster blocks sit well and the grids left behind after cutting stay in shape. They are slightly less 'forgiving' than linen when it comes to some of the pulled thread techniques, which rely on creating holes for effect, but, with care, the right results can be achieved. For those who find 28 threads to the inch rather tiring on the eyes, the Lugana is an excellent alternative as the resulting lacy effects are close to those worked on the finer fabric. There is an interesting colour range in all fabrics.

Obviously, I could not use every evenweave fabric that is on the market, and there may well be some that are your favourites that I have

not used, such as the evenweave cotton fabric called Hardanger or Oslo fabric. This fabric is woven with 22 double threads to the inch, which is used as one thread. It is thicker than other evenweaves, which means that the finished Hardanger looks more solid and geometric. The choice is yours but, if you substitute Hardanger or Oslo fabric for any of the projects in this book, the finished piece will look more chunky and allowances will have to be made to accommodate the finished larger size.

Threads

You will need two thicknesses of thread for any Hardanger project. Kloster blocks, surface motifs and border stitches will be worked with the thicker thread; needleweaving, pulled thread stitches (eyelets, reversed diagonal faggoting, hem stitching and edgings) and infilling stitches with the finer thread.

Coton Perlé is now widely used, being not only suitable but readily available. Coton Perlé comes in many shades and varying thicknesses, and the one to choose is determined by the number of threads in the fabric being used. For fabrics with a 24-count or less, No. 5 is more appropriate for the kloster blocks. For fabrics with a 25- and 26-count, there is a choice of No. 5 or No. 8 for the blocks. This is a matter of preference in addition to the texture of the fabric. For fabrics with a 27- to 32-count, it is preferable to stitch the kloster blocks with No. 8. Use No. 12 on fabrics with a finer count than 32. The two sizes of thread

required to complete most of the projects in this book are Coton Perlé Nos. 8 and 12. In some instances you will not require a whole ball of pearl cotton as specified in the materials list and you will be able to use the remainder in another project.

Sometimes shades found in Nos. 5 and 8 are not available in No. 12, which is very frustrating when you need a No. 8 and No. 12 to match. In these circumstances two threads of a matching stranded cotton (generally less difficult to obtain) may be substituted. Take care with the needleweaving to ensure the threads lie flat and do not cross over each other.

Linen thread (traditionally used, but now not so readily available) could also be worked. To decide the correct thickness, withdraw a thread from your fabric and lay it beside your sewing threads. Your stitching thread for the heavier work should be slightly thicker than the background thread, and slightly thinner for the finer work. Do not forget to make your own quantity allowances for these differences if you work with linen thread.

All the Hardanger projects in this book could be worked with another choice of thread. Don't be afraid to experiment for yourself. There is a wonderfully exciting assortment of multicoloured or space-dyed threads in varying thicknesses now available. Choose the correct thickness as above but check that your choice of thread is colourfast, as it would be ruinous otherwise.

Think carefully before making your choice of colours, which must depend on the effect you require. Multicolour embroidery does not always result in the look you think

you are going to achieve. When joining subsequent space-dyed threads, do remember to cut from the same end of the skein, allowing the colours to follow on. I suggest that you work a small practice piece first so you can be certain you like the effect.

Although multicolours have crept into contemporary Hardanger embroidery, it must be remembered that the appeal of Hardanger lies in the negative and the positive effect. The importance of delicate openwork patterns and fillings against dense and textured outlines is shown off to perfection using white on white. Multicolours are fun but need to be used carefully and with a purpose. They can dominate the Hardanger design so that the effect of the openwork pattern is lost, and the Hardanger merely becomes surface stitchery. Try to choose threads that have a relationship to the background fabric.

When I use colours in Hardanger I find that the best results for pulled thread techniques such as reversed diagonal faggoting are achieved using the same colour thread as the background. This is a stitch that relies totally on small, tightly pulled holes for effect and this is easily destroyed with contrasting or multicolours.

In this book I have used a selection from the Caron Collection Wildflowers, which is similar to flower thread or No.8/12 pearl cotton and also Oliver Twist dyed thread, which is found in a combination skein of matching 8s and 12s.

I could not resist using a few metallic threads, such as DMC Fil Argent Clair and Kreinik's Fine Braid and Blending Filament.

Metallics are not quite as easy to use as cotton, but if you are careful they will give you the effect you are looking for. Do not have your thread too long as it may shred. The Blending Filament is generally used with another thread so that there is 'lift' rather than 'dominance', and it is particularly effective in Hardanger. All these metallics come in shades of gold and silver.

Equipment

For all the projects you will need the following basic equipment:

- Have a good quality pair of embroidery scissors, with fine, sharp points that cut 'to the point'. This is essential for cutting the threads and giving the cut work a neat appearance.

- Use blunt-ended tapestry needles size 24 or 26 with your two sizes of thread.

- It is not necessary to use an embroidery hoop as it restricts your stitching movement. It can also become irritating to be constantly moving it from one area to the next. If you prefer to work with a frame, make sure it is bound and use a piece of soft fabric inside the hoop against the work to prevent squashing or distorting stitches already worked.

- You will need some pastel coloured tacking thread.

TECHNIQUES

Preparing to Work

1 Neaten the edges of the linen by pulling a thread and cutting straight along this line.

2 Oversew or machine zigzag the linen edges to prevent fraying.

3 To find the centre of the fabric, fold it in half and crease gently, first in one direction and then the other.

4 Instructions with the projects will tell you when to tack in the central, horizontal and vertical lines with a line of basting stitches in a pastel coloured thread.

5 To keep your Hardanger clean, store in a protective bag or pillowcase.

To Start and Finish Off Your Thread

1 Use a waste knot. Secure the thread with an away waste knot

on the surface of the linen, 7.5 cm (3 in) away to the side of your initial stitch. Once the stitches are completed, cut off the knot, rethread the tail of cotton and weave through the back of the completed stitches, taking two or three small back stitches to secure.

2 As a general rule, to fasten off, go to the back and slip through the completed stitches, fixing with a few small back stitches.

Understanding the Projects

1 Work methodically.

2 If you are having difficulty with the counting and placing of kloster blocks in some of the larger projects, run tacking guidelines across the fabric once you have completed the first kloster block. Work in bands of 24 threads, in both directions, so that you have a grid of tacking lines to help you match up kloster blocks on the opposite side of any design.

Altering the Project Dimensions

1 All the projects may easily be worked on any fabric count other than the ones suggested, as the final dimensions can be altered to suit your preferences and the fabric.

2 If you work on a fabric with a lesser count than the one specified in the projects, the dimensions will change

accordingly and the finished item will be bigger. It is necessary, therefore, to make the relevant allowance for extra fabric.

3 If the fabric count is higher than the one specified in the projects, the finished item will be finer and smaller. All the projects may be worked on thread counts between 25 and 28 without making major differences to the size of the finished item.

4 Adjustments to the size of the place mat, table napkin and bread-basket cloth may be made by altering the number of kloster blocks in the straight lines between each corner. If you want a larger cloth, add more blocks; for a smaller one, do not work so many. Remember, however, to do the same on each side.

5 To make a set of table napkins or place mats, always cut all of them at the same time and all going the same way, with the selvage running in the same direction.

Fillings

1 Most of the fillings are inter-changeable and you can make your own choices if you prefer.

2 Where there is a single diagonal line of needleweaving, picot knots, picot loops or half Greek cross filling may be used. Consider the effect before combining different stitches.

3 Where there is more than one diagonal line of needleweaving

forming squares in the design, picot knots, picot loops, square filets, dove's eye or loop filling, spider's web and half Greek crosses may be substituted for each other. Combinations of filling stitches may be made; however, I always prefer to leave the squares on the edge of the design free of fillings. This emphasizes the negative and positive, and thus shows up the central design so that it looks delicate and lacy, but crisp and uncluttered at the sides.

4 If you feel you would like to tackle a project but are rather daunted by the filling, you can simplify the design by just working plain needleweaving without ornamentation – it will still look impressive.

Charts

1 Each line represents one thread of fabric.

2 For the smaller projects the chart shows all the design.

3 For the larger projects a quarter or repeat is shown and it will be necessary to work the reverse side.

4 Small dark arrow marks on the edges of the chart denote the centre lines.

5 All the charts show you where to start the kloster blocks, needleweaving and fillings so that you proceed consistently. The number of stitches shown on the bars is an average number and is

merely a guide to the procedure. You may require more or fewer, depending on how tightly you pull the threads and what fabric count you are using.

6 Keys to charts denote the stitches and which thread to use.

Washing Completed Work

1 Do not wash either your threads or fabric until you have completed the whole project.

2 Carefully wash your finished embroidery by hand using a mild soap powder. Rinse well. Dry, face down, on towelling, stretch carefully into shape and press when damp on the back.

STITCHES

Traditional Hardanger embroidery is characterized by satin stitch blocks (Klostersaum) formed into geometric designs, and the cutting and withdrawal of threads within these shapes. The resulting grid is embroidered and embellished with needleweaving (Stoppesaum) and lacy infilling stitches, thereby making it stronger as well as decorative. More ornate filling stitches enhance the lacy effects. Further embellishment of traditional solid satin stitch motifs (e.g. stars and diamonds) counter the lacy effects to give depth and substance to the geometric designs.

Basic stitches and techniques are incorporated in the small designs given in this chapter. Work the

samplers to familiarize yourself with Hardanger stitches before working any other projects. The designs will help you practise your tension and give you a 'feel' for the threads and fabric. Because they are small and quick, it is not the end of the world if you make a mistake or cut the wrong thread. You will also discover that Hardanger embroidery is hugely satisfying to do and not nearly as alarming and complicated as you perhaps thought.

These small samplers will give you confidence to go on and work any of the designs in the book and, if you are pleased with the results, they could be turned into something practical such as an insert for a birthday card, a needlecase, a mat, a paperweight or a pincushion. After working the first two samples, you might like to combine elements from each piece to create your own personal design.

Although the traditional white thread on white fabric always looks beautiful, for these very first projects, choose a pastel background fabric (e.g. the DMC Lugana 25-count) with white thread so that you can see exactly what you are doing. The charts and working instructions are at the end of the chapter (see pages 38–43). The Norwegian translation of stitches is shown in brackets.

The first practice sampler (see page 38) incorporates kloster blocks (on the straight and diagonally), square and diagonal eyelets, reversed diagonal faggoting, basic eight-pointed star, wrapped and woven bars and an outline of twisted lattice band.

Kloster Blocks (Klostersaum)

Worked in straight rows or diagonally at right angles to each other, kloster blocks consist of five straight stitches worked side by side over four threads of the fabric (Fig. 1). They outline the design and are always worked with the thicker thread.

1 Start with an away waste knot on the surface (see pages 15–16) with a thread that is slightly longer than usual because it is quickly used up.

2 Come up through the fabric at A and take a stitch over four threads as shown, always working the stitches in each block in the same direction. Being consistent will eliminate any problems when the fabric is cut. Stitches may be

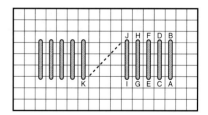

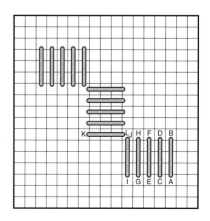

Fig.1 Kloster blocks

stabbed or sewn (down and up through the fabric in one movement), but always go through the holes in the fabric and try not to split any fabric threads.

3 Always start and finish your thread at one end of a block and not in the middle. The new thread tends to be crisper and shinier, and sometimes there is a noticeable difference between the old and new if you see it closely side by side.

4 Pull the stitch to sit comfortably on the surface of the fabric, but not so tightly that it bunches up and distorts the fabric threads.

5 As you sew your design, keep checking that the kloster blocks are lined up correctly (in all directions) and that you have not miscounted somewhere. This saves a lot of heartache later on. Tacking lines from one side of the design to the other will help you to see whether you are correct.

6 To finish off kloster blocks, take the thread to the back and slip through the 'tunnels' formed by the blocks. Come up through the second block and take a back stitch over the middle thread. Hold the block and pull tightly to set the stitch firmly in position. Repeat the process in the next block and, to ensure the thread is secure before cutting off, extend the 'tail' through one more block.

7 Once you have established some blocks, you will be able to start a new thread in the same way you finished it, but take care to hold the previous thread tail firmly as you pull through the new one so that it is not pulled out of the block. Always do your new securing back stitches in a 'clean' block with no other back stitches.

8 Always outline the design completely with the kloster blocks before going on to any other part of the design.

9 Do not be afraid to turn the work if you find this to be a more comfortable way of working.

Square Eyelet (Dronningsting)

Eyelets are not only decorative, but when used with buttonhole edging help to strengthen the edges (Fig. 2). The starting point of eyelets is very important and makes the difference between their being evenly formed all the way round or lopsided and bulky where the last stitch is made.

Fig.2 Square eyelet

1 Using the fine thread, stitch eyelets over two threads. Start with a waste knot and work clockwise.

2 Although eyelets can be started in various places, for perfect eyelets that are even all the way round bring the needle up from the outside edge at A (just one hole to the right of the centre line of the eyelet) and down through the centre hole at B.

3 Hold the eyelet and pull the thread gently away from the centre towards the edge to form a hole. Repeat the process until the eyelet is complete.

4 For eyelets with buttonhole edging, complete the first eyelet and move to subsequent eyelets by slipping the threads through the blocks (on the wrong side). Start each successive eyelet at the same point, but one square further on.

5 For a half eyelet, begin stitching one side of the eyelet and work as shown (Fig. 2).

6 To ensure the fine thread is securely started and finished off, take the thread to the wrong side (pulling away from the last stitch and centre hole) and go through the already completed stitches or blocks. Anchor the thread with a back stitch through one stitch of a kloster block, hold the block, pull tightly and repeat to prevent it slipping. As the thread is fine, extend the 'tail' through three subsequent blocks.

Diagonal Eyelets

Diagonal eyelets (Fig. 3) are delicate and decorative when they are used beside a heavier motif, giving an open, lacy look to the work. And they are not as difficult to work as they look.

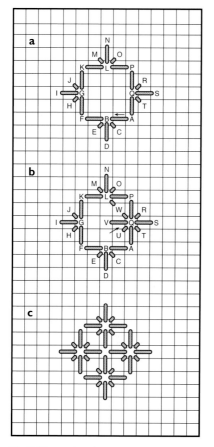

Fig.3 Diagonal eyelet

1 Using the fine thread, work eyelets over two threads starting at A. Stitch down into the centre hole of the stitch and pull gently away from the middle to the sides as you proceed round.

2 Stitch around the outside of all four eyelets in a clockwise direction (Fig. 3a). Start at A > B and proceed: C > B, D > B, E > B, F > B back to F; F > G and

continue to K > G back to K; K > L and continue to P > L back to P; P > Q, R > Q, S > Q, T > Q, A > Q.

3 When you reach Q, continue to work around the inside of the eyelet (Fig. 3b), stitching anticlockwise, U > Q, V > Q, W > Q back to W. Stitch W > L and complete (Fig. 3c).

Reversed Diagonal Faggoting Stitch (Vestmannarenning)

This pulled thread stitch (Fig. 4), with its 'open' effect, works beautifully as an outline definition to the kloster blocks. Practise this stitch on some spare fabric to get the feel for it before using it in a project.

1 Figs. 4a and b show two different starting positions, depending on whether you are working a diagonal line or mitred points. Secure your thread and bring your needle up through the fabric, commencing at 1 and using the fine thread.

2 Work diagonally over two threads as shown, for the required number of stitches.

3 For the return journey, turn the work upside-down and repeat the stitch as before, going over the centre line a second time. Don't be afraid to turn the work if it is a more comfortable working method and you will see that you are looking at the stitch in the same way that you started.

4 Pull gently after each stitch (away from the centre hole) to create the 'open' effect, holding the stitch so that the fabric does not twist. Make sure that the threads lie side by side and not on top of each other. It is especially important to achieve the 'open' effect because the stitch completely loses its impact if it is just sitting on the surface as solid diagonal lines.

5 Check that your stitches line up opposite each other in all directions and with the kloster blocks.

Figs.4a–b Reversed diagonal faggotting

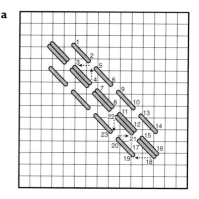

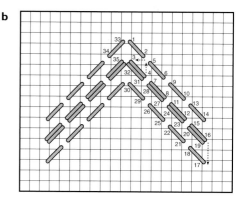

Satin Stitch Star (Åttebladsrose)

Stars (Figs. 5a–c) are characteristic of traditional Hardanger embroidery and are one of the most important and most used motifs in this technique. Against the the lacy effects of other stitches, these solid motifs add texture and depth to the designs. With a simple additional flourish added to the top of the star, as shown, they become the ship or tulip motif (Fig. 5c). The number and size of stitches in these motifs are often changed and adapted to fit a particular design, but the basic shape and method for working remain the same as for working the star. Eyelets are often added in the 'arms' or at the centre of the star to create an effective contrast.

I Start at 1, working with the thicker thread.

2 Complete one point as shown in Fig. 5a, take the thread through to the back and come up to the front at 23.

Figs.5a–c Satin stitch star

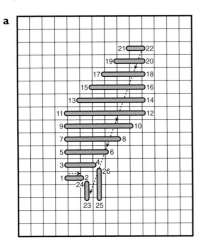

3 Complete the process to form a half or whole star (Fig. 5b).

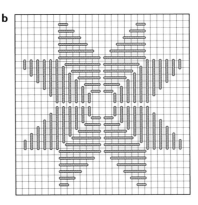

4 Add on the extra stitches (Fig. 5c) if you are working the ship motif.

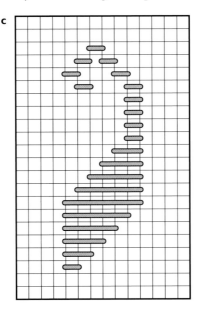

5 Always stitch a motif separately and do not carry threads from one motif to another.

6 Where possible, when stitches share the same hole, stab down into the hole to keep the threads lying smoothly and try not to pull your satin stitches too tightly.

7 If appropriate, work a square eyelet in the centre of the star.

Cutting and Withdrawal of Threads (Utskårsøm)

Don't be afraid to cut. After the threads have been cut, you will be left with a grid of four threads to needleweave. Complete the kloster blocks and all other surface embroidery before you cut any part of the design (Figs.6a–b).

I Cut your four threads against the sides of your satin stitches and never at the 'open' end of the block.

2 When cutting the threads, position the scissors to the left of the satin stitches forming the kloster block (Fig. 6a).

Figs.6a–b Cutting fabric threads

3 Adjust the threads to be cut on the blades of the scissors, and check you have the right number before cutting all four together. Never cut one at a time because you can easily snip an extra thread by mistake.

4 Cut one side of the design, turn the work and repeat the process on the opposite side (Fig.6b).

5 Pull out the cut threads carefully. The remaining threads must be wrapped or woven.

b

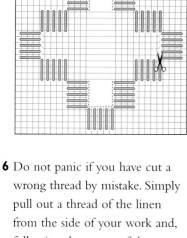

6 Do not panic if you have cut a wrong thread by mistake. Simply pull out a thread of the linen from the side of your work and, following the weave of the cut thread, darn and reweave your new thread into position beside the one you have snipped. Then needleweave or wrap these two threads as one until they are secured.

Needleweaving (Stoppestingsstaver)

The finer thread is used for weaving, and it is important for needlewoven bars (Figs. 7a–b) to be tightly woven, uniform and straight. Woven bars tend to keep their square shape better than wrapped bars do, and decorative French knots or picots can be added.

I Either come through to the front, having anchored the thread through the back of the kloster blocks, or secure the thread with a waste knot, which is positioned as shown in Fig. 7a on the surface of the work.

2 Bring the thread diagonally from behind and to the left of the bar, into the open square.

Figs.7a–b Starting thread to weave a bar

a

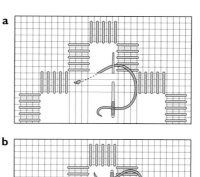

b

3 Place the needle down into the middle of the bar with the point facing up and over the new thread (Fig.7a). 'Cast' the needle so that it now points down and the thread is trapped (Fig.7b). The needle is now in position to continue weaving, with three threads on one side and two on the other. The extra thread will be woven with the two on the left side of the bar. Once the bar is woven, cut off the knot and continue with the next bar. The advantages of this method are that there are fewer 'ends' being worked through the back of the kloster blocks and therefore less bulk and, if you have to, you can start in the middle of a design.

4 Weave the bars by taking the needle down into the middle of the bar, weaving under and over two threads at a time in a figure of eight (Fig. 8a). Hold the threads under your thumb as you do each stitch and pull tightly towards the start or woven end of the bar to achieve bars which have a neat and even tension.

Figs.8a–b Needleweaving the bars

a

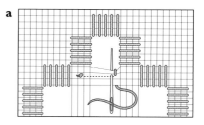

5 Aim to complete the same number of stitches on each bar so the grid does not become distorted. Do not cram too many stitches on each bar.

6 On completing a bar, progress to the next one, taking the needle behind from the far side of the completed bar, down into the centre of the next bar (Fig. 8b). You may find it easier to hold your fabric at a slight angle when you weave the bars.

b

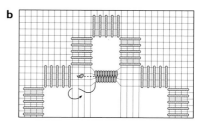

7 Work consistently diagonally down across the design, in steps, and not from bar to bar in the same row. Try to stitch each diagonal row from right to left and, on reaching the last bar, finish off the thread to start again at the top right of the next row to be worked. If you keep to this method, any filling stitches stitched with the needleweaving will all be worked in the same way in the design and any crossed corners will correspond accordingly.

8 Always try to ensure you have enough thread to reach and finish off in a kloster block. If you misjudge and have to end the thread in the middle of the design, bring the old thread up to the surface at the next intersection as shown in Fig. 9.

Fig.9 Ending the thread on a bar

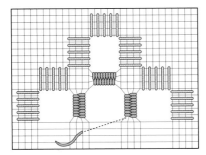

Wrapped or Overcast Bars (Overkasting av staver)

Although wrapped or overcast bars (Figs. 10a–c) are thinner and can be stitched more quickly than woven bars, it is harder to keep them straight and well lined up. However, when they are used advisedly they create another dimension to Hardanger embroidery. Knots or picots cannot be worked on wrapped bars.

I Wrapping may be worked horizontally or vertically (depending on how you prefer to hold the fabric), and it is worked with the finer thread. Avoid overlapping the stitches and gently hold each stitch as it is wrapped so that you are in control of the tension.

2 Secure the thread safely with one or two back stitches in the kloster blocks behind the direction in which you will be travelling. Then bring the thread up from underneath the bar to be worked (Fig. 10a). This will enable the first stitch to be pulled tightly into the corner of the bar and determine the tension of the wrapping.

Figs.10a–c Overcast bars

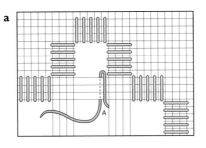

3 Wrap the bar tightly and consistently, from the bottom of the bar to the top, but do not cram too many stitches on each bar otherwise they will distort.

4 Progress from behind the (horizontal) first bar and over the top of the next (vertical) bar (Fig. 10b) to wrap from right to left. Complete this bar and come up from behind the subsequent bar to wrap from bottom to top as before.

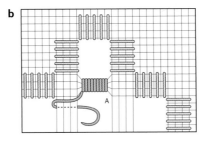

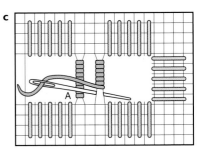

5 To complete large areas it is preferable to wrap all the vertical bars and then all the horizontal bars in order to keep the lines straight, but make sure that you are wrapping consistently in the same direction. Threads may be divided and wrapped (Fig.10c).

6 If you are travelling from bar to bar through kloster blocks, to continue with the correct method of wrapping, it may be necessary to slip the thread through a kloster block that is behind the direction you are going. Take the thread over a single thread of the block in order to travel forwards again, ready to wrap the bar and be in a position to pull the first stitch tightly into the corner of the new bar as before.

7 If you have to end a thread in the middle of a design, follow the instructions as shown in Fig.9. Start your new thread with a knot on the surface at one intersection to the side of the way you were travelling, and bring the thread underneath the subsequent bar ready to wrap again.

8 It may be necessary to reverse the way a bar is wrapped to suit a design. This is acceptable as long as you continue in a consistent manner.

Twisted Lattice Band (Kjederand)

This decorative stitch (Figs. 11a–c) gives the appearance of a delicate braid and is often used to border collars and cuffs of the shirts worn with the Hardanger bunad.

1 Secure and start with the thicker thread to form your cross stitches, using the method of working a row of diagonal stitches from right to left over four threads (Fig. 11a), and returning in the opposite direction (Fig. 11b). Pull each stitch tightly, but not so tightly that it causes holes and 'dragging' in the fabric. It is important for this foundation line of crosses to be firm enough to hold the lacing to create a crisp, fluted edge and not an untidy wobbly edge.

Figs. 11a–c Twisted lattice band

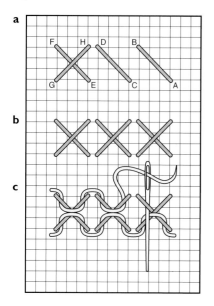

2 The surface lacing is woven in two journeys on top of the crossed stitches, as shown in Fig. 11c, working from right to left for the bottom row and in the opposite direction for the top row.

Progressing to the second sampler is merely an extension to your skills (see page 40). There are a few eyelets to keep your hand in and you will already be familiar with the kloster blocks, reversed diagonal faggoting and twisted lattice band. The design has been altered slightly to include more cutting, needleweaving practice and a simple picot knot on the bars. You have the choice of either picots, a spider's web or loop/dove's eye filling in the central diamond shape and the opportunity to mitre the reversed diagonal faggoting which is one my favourite effects in Hardanger.

Woven Bars with Picot Knots (Stoppestingsstaver med knuter)

A woven bar with picot knots (Fig. 12) on one or both sides adds to the delicacy of a decorative filling or 'softens' the lines of a woven grid.

1 Needleweave to the centre of the bar with the finer thread.

2 In a clockwise direction, wrap the thread twice around the needle, before placing the needle down into the middle of the bar to work the next stitch. Hold the knot firmly in position while

pulling the needle and thread through the centre to finish needleweaving the rest of the bar. Try not to jerk the thread, because this can move the knot out of place.

Fig. 12 Woven bars with picot knots

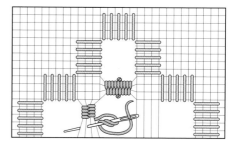

3 For a picot on both sides of the bar, complete the first knot and take the thread to the opposite side in the normal way. Turn the work so that the first knot sits on the left side of the bar and work the second picot in the same manner before completing the rest of the needleweaving.

Woven Bars with Looped Picots

Looped picots (Figs. 13–15) are open knots formed in the middle of woven bars, and they give a more ornate lacy look to the embroidery. They should not be worked in squares that will contain other fillings because most of the small square will be taken up with the loops.

1 Needleweave to the centre of the bar with the finer thread. To make the loop picot, insert half of the needle between the fabric threads following the direction of the last stitch (Fig. 13a).

2 Slip the thread under and over the needle point to form a loop (Fig. 13b).

Figs. 13a–c Bars with picot loops (looped on left)

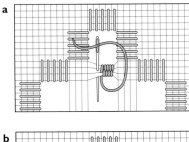

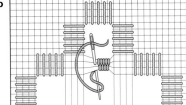

3 Pull the needle and thread through the rest of the bar and loop, gently down and back towards the woven end (Fig. 13c). Do not pull too tightly otherwise your loop will become a knot.

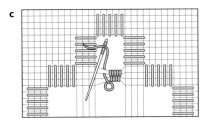

4 Take the needle back into the middle of the bar, gently pulling the thread across the bar towards the unwoven end. Bring the thread back in line towards the base and, holding the loop picot and bar between your finger and thumb, pull the thread firmly down to anchor the knot at the side of the bar.

5 Continue weaving the rest of the bar unless you are going to make a loop on the opposite side, in which case the process is exactly the same but in the opposite direction (Figs. 14a–c).

Fig. 14a Bars with picot loops (looped on right)

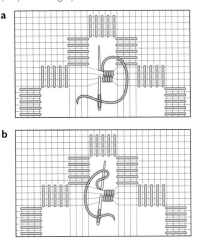

6 As there are no crossed-over threads in this filling, it is possible to work up and down the diagonal lines in a design working the picot loops as you advance.

Fig. 15 Bars with picot loops (looped both sides)

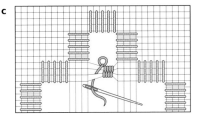

Spider's Web Filling (Edderkoppfylling)

The spider's web filling (Figs. 16a–c) gives the effect of a diagonal cross spanning a cut square with a small spider's web in the centre. It may be used with wrapped or woven bars.

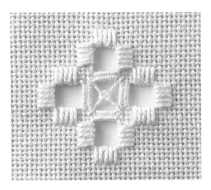

1 Work three sides of a square before starting the spider's web filling.

2 Come through to the surface at A. Taking the thread diagonally across the open square, come up from the back at B (Fig. 16a).

Figs. 16a–c Spider's web filling

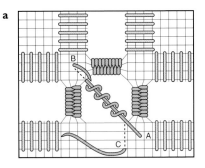

3 Take the thread back across towards A, wrapping the thread three or four times around the thread AB. (The number of wraps will depend on the the thickness of thread and fabric being used.

Don't overdo the wrapping.) Pull the twisted thread towards A and, holding the stitch, carefully tighten it to adjust the tension to fit the square so that the spider's web will be firmly balanced.

4 Bring the thread underneath the horizontal bar and needleweave the fourth and final bar of the square starting at C (Fig. 16a).

5 Come through to the surface at D, taking the thread diagonally across the open square again to come up from the back at E (Fig. 16b).

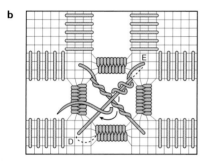

b

6 Wrap this diagonal thread DE once or twice, taking the needle underneath the middle intersection. Adjust the twists by holding the threads and pulling firmly towards D.

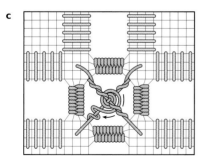

c

7 Form the centre wheel by passing the needle over this top diagonal

thread and under the next, moving round in a circle and repeating the process (Fig.16c). Adjust and pull to ensure the first circle joins the two crossed diagonal threads together.

8 Continue in a clockwise direction, following the weaving of the first circle, until you have finished two or three more complete circles. The threads are not pulled tightly as they are woven, but adjust them at the end of each circle.

9 Always try to remember how many rings you have made in the circle if you are working a series because it is important that they all look the same size.

10 To finish off at the end of the last circle, wrap the thread around the diagonal twist DE once or twice more, pulling the first wrap back carefully, but tightly towards the centre so that it has a neat finish. Make an extra wrap if necessary, but remember to hold the stitch as you do this so you do not distort it. Pull the last wrap away from the web to tighten it. Taking the thread diagonally under the intersection of fabric threads at D, come up to the surface to the left of the bar ready to needleweave.

Loop or Dove's Eye Filling (Spindel)

Loop or dove's eye filling (Figs. 17a–b) is an open lacy filling stitch which may be used with either wrapped or woven bars. A

development of this stitch is used to fill large areas where the bars are unworked. The resulting mesh is not only attractive, but also strengthens the area which has had threads withdrawn.

1 It is important that all four sides of the dove's eye should cross in the same way and they can be worked either clockwise or anticlockwise.

2 Complete the needleweaving on three and a half sides of a square of withdrawn threads before starting the dove's eye filling.

Figs. 17a–b Loop or dove's eye filling

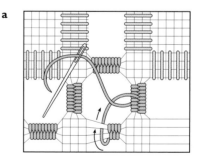

a

3 For a dove's eye worked anticlockwise, come up into the middle of the square and stab down into the centre of the needlewoven bar to the right (Fig. 17a).

4 Bring the thread up from underneath, loop over the first thread, and down into the centre of the next bar.

5 Adjust the shape and repeat the process to the last bar.

6 To finish, slip the thread under the first loop and back down into the middle (Fig. 17b) to continue needleweaving the last half of the bar, readjusting the shape if necessary, before completion. Try to make the dove's eyes all the same size and do not pull them too tightly.

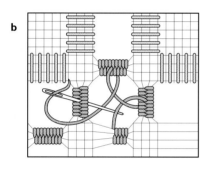
b

7 Reverse the process for working dove's eyes in a clockwise direction.

The third sampler (see page 42) shows you how to work a buttonhole edging on the diagonal so that ultimately the work may be cut away from the background. There is more reversed diagonal faggoting, eyelets (used not only for effect but also to strengthen the edge) and you are introduced to the square filet filling stitch although you may prefer to work a filling of your own choice. You might find that you want to repeat this design and practise some of the other filling stitches that follow in this chapter. Work two and turn it into a pot-pourri sachet for a perfect present.

Buttonhole Stitch Edging (Tungesting)

This loop stitch (Figs. 18a–d) is used to outline and enclose the edge of a design so that embroidery may be cut away from the background. Not only practical, but decorative as well, it can also be used to give density and depth to an inner part of the design.

1 If there is an inner row of kloster blocks, work these before the buttonhole edging.

2 Secure the thread with a waste knot and work from left to right. Come up through the fabric at A, taking the needle down at B, one thread to the right of A and four threads up.

3 Before pulling tightly, come up at C within the loop AB (Fig. 18a). Pull up to lie neatly on the surface.

Figs. 18a–d Buttonhole stitch edging

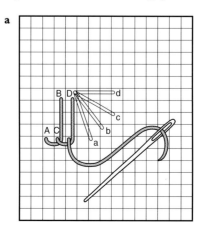
a

4 To turn a corner, follow Figs. 18a and 18b. Leave a space before coming up at a. Work three buttonhole stitches on the diagonal at a, b and c, going down into the corner hole (marked with a dot) each time. Leave another space before coming up at d, to start the next block of buttonhole stitches. Five threads will be packed into the corner hole, so try not to pull too tightly and enlarge the area.

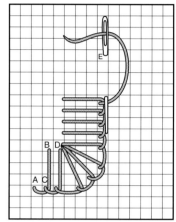
b

5 Always check that you have made the correct positioning of stitches at a, b, c and d. If it is difficult to find the right holes, gently push the previous stitch to one side to get your bearings.

6 For a right-angled corner (Fig. 18c) bring your needle up through the fabric at E before forming a loop and continuing with the stitch.

7 To start a new thread, follow Fig. 18c. It is important not to see any joins, so make the link in the middle of a block. Leave the old short thread to one side and join in a new one weaving through the back, taking one or two back stitches to secure. Bring the needle through at Y and make a buttonhole loop in the next space. Continue stitching. When you have finished the working thread, return to the loose thread at the join and 'missing' stitch. Take this thread under the small beginning loop of the working thread and down into the fabric at Z (Fig. 18d). Fasten off at the back of the work.

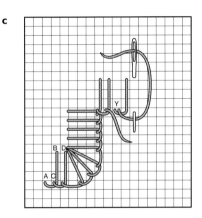

c

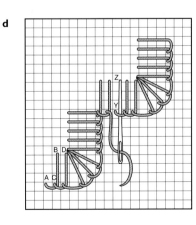

d

8 If buttonhole edging is going to be worked in a straight line, it is advisable to machine stitch a small zigzag along the line before buttonholing to strengthen the edge.

9 Complete the embroidery, wash and press before cutting the fabric away from the buttonhole stitch. I prefer to cut after washing, because if you are working with something very small it is useful to have some fabric to hold, and stretch if necessary, when pressing.

10 Cut the fabric threads carefully from the back, in case one or two buttonhole stitches are not correctly positioned. To cut, nestle the scissor point in the 'ditch' between fabric and buttonhole edge and try not to cut the buttonhole loops on the right side by mistake. It is not the end of the world if you do, but it is a nuisance to have to unravel the cut thread and redo the buttonhole edging. Cut each thread individually at the corners.

Square Filet Filling (Skråspindel)

Used with either woven or wrapped bars, square filet filling (Fig. 19a–b) is an open, lacy filling stitch. It is particularly effective when worked over larger open areas as a secondary pattern appears giving the effect of each square being outlined by a 'halo' or circle.

1 In a design, stitch the square filets in the same direction so that the corners all cross in the same manner. They may be worked clockwise or anticlockwise.

2 Weave or wrap all four sides of the square before stitching the square filets with the finer thread.

3 Bring the needle through to the surface at A in the centre of the fabric corner enclosing the open squares. Taking the thread into the open square, come up in the corner at B (Fig. 19a). Adjust the loop by pulling away from A.

Fig. 19a–b Square filet filling

a

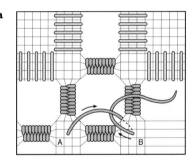

4 Move to the next corner by taking the thread into the open square again, underneath the loop AB and up from underneath at C (Fig. 19b). Adjust the loop by pulling away from B and repeat the process to the last stitch.

b

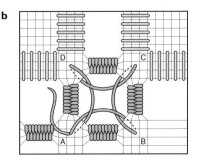

5 Complete the last part of the filet by taking your needle under loop CD and over loop AB. Either come up to the surface at A and take a small diagonal back stitch (hold and pull tightly to hide it underneath the first loop thread) to anchor the thread and 'keep the line' before finishing off, or continue diagonally across under the corner ready to weave the next bar.

6 Adjust all the loops to achieve a good square shape before finishing off or moving on to the next bar.

Extra Fillings, Stitches, Hems and Edgings

The extra fillings, stitches and techniques that follow will be found in other projects throughout the book. The fillings are just as easy and fun to do, work well in different shapes and could be used as alternatives to the ones already discussed. Four different methods are shown for hems and edgings.

Greek Cross Filling

Greek cross filling (Figs. 20a–d) is a useful and effective decorative filling, which can be used in a variety of combinations. Impressive as a single motif, it will also give a textured 'rippling' effect when used on the diagonal.

1 Wrap the bars, divided in half (with the finer thread) and starting at A to the left of the bar (Fig. 20a). Work towards the centre of the square wrapping over from left to right.

Figs. 20a–d Greek Cross Filling

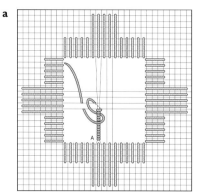

a

2 To travel to the next bar, take the thread underneath the centre intersection, up through the middle of the four threads and over the second bar. Pull this first stitch firmly towards the centre hole to tighten it (Fig. 20a).

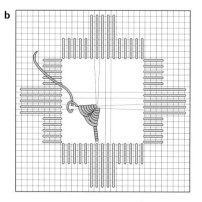

b

3 In a figure-of-eight method, weave under and over these bars. The first stitches should be pulled tightly and should gradually get looser to achieve the fan shape. Continue until you have the stitch

the size you require and remember to note the number of wraps you have worked on each side (Fig.20b).

4 Following the same motion, finish wrapping the first group of two fabric threads on the second bar.

5 To move to the second group of fabric threads, take the needle underneath and come up on the far side at B (Fig. 20c). Repeating the process, wrap the threads as before.

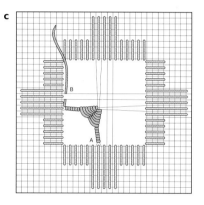

c

6 Complete the rest of the motif to form the whole Greek cross filling.

7 To finish off at the end of the last bar and to keep the ends together, take the thread behind and wrap the first and last, pull tightly and anchor the thread in the kloster blocks.

8 To fill an open area the crosses will have to be worked diagonally, one side of the cross at a time, as shown in Fig. 20d. Turn the work to make the return journey and complete the other half of the crosses.

d

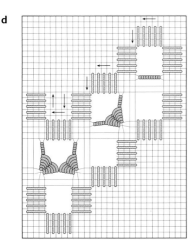

Diagonal Twisted Bars and Picot Knot Filling (Skrå staver med knuter)

This is a much used and basic filling combination. Many of the more elaborate patterns (not shown in this book) are based on this traditional mixture of stitches.

1 For a single motif the bars will need to be woven as shown by the directional arrows (Fig. 21a) using the finer thread.

2 Anchor the thread as described in the section on needleweaving, step 1 (see page 21) but with the knot in the centre X so that you can start the weaving from the side, working to the centre of the motif and across to the other side.

Figs. 21a–b Diagonal twisted bars with picot knot filling

a

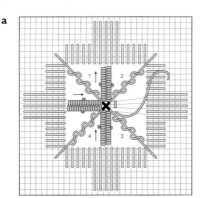

3 Weave three of the bars, working the picots on both sides of the bars as you proceed, and then bring the needle up in the centre hole X.

4 Work a twisted spoke diagonally across each of the open squares in order starting in square No. 1 (refer to the spider's web filling, step 2 on page 24) and come up into the centre hole after each twisted bar.

5 Complete the last twisted spoke and bring the needle up above the last bar ready to finish the weaving.

b

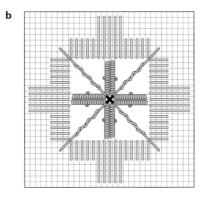

6 Finish off the thread in a kloster block as usual.

Simple Star

This simple star of satin stitches is smaller than the familiar 'åttebladsrose' (satin stitch star) and will fit neatly into small sections of any Hardanger design. Eyelets are often added to lighten the density of the satin stitches.

Fig. 22 Simple star

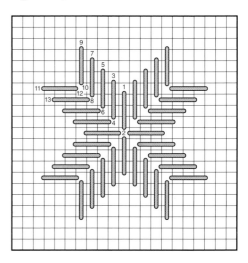

1 Work the simple star using the thicker thread.

2 Start with a waste knot and come to the surface at 1 (see Fig. 22) and work a straight satin stitch over four threads.

3 Follow the numbered sequence and progress round the whole motif.

4 Finish off both thread ends in the the back of the motif taking one or two back stitches over a single thread.

5 If eyelets are to be included, refer to the relevant chart in the book to see the positioning.

Hem Turnings and Edgings

Hems can be finished off using a variety of methods, which must be suitable for the project you are working. If your finished item is intended to undergo a lot of washing, ensure that you choose the correct hem to withstand the wear and tear and not one that will fray and unravel after the first wash.

Always leave at least 5 cm (2 in) for the hem turnings, depending on the fabric count. A lower count fabric may require a wider hem, and therefore more threads in the width, to balance the work.

Preparing to Hem and Mitre Corners (Hjørner)

Hems can be sewn either to the front or the back of the work depending on preferences. If turned to the front, there is more of a ridge on the surface than if the hem is turned to the back. It is important to have crisp, right-angled mitred corners that do not have a little bulge at the tip.

I Tack a thread along the line that the hem stitch is going to be worked (Fig. 23a). Sometimes threads are withdrawn on this line so that a ladder hem stitch may be worked to create a more open border effect.

2 Make a second tacking line after counting the required number of threads (e.g. 12 threads) that will make up the width of the hem. This will become the outside fold line.

Figs. 23a–c

Preparing fabric for a hem and to mitre corners

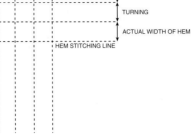

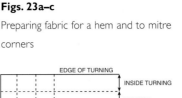

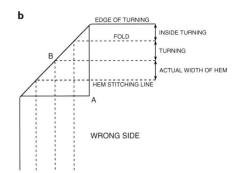

3 Tack a third line exactly the same number of threads away as for the first side of the hem (e.g. 12 threads). This will become the inside fold line.

4 Trim the excess fabric one thread less (e.g. 11 threads) than the chosen width of the hem. This part will be turned right inside the hem and cutting it a thread less ensures that the inner piece of fabric sits flat inside the hem and does not curl over on the fold line.

5 Turn and tack the hem into position and mitre the corners as follows.

6 To mitre the corner (Fig. 23b), fold the fabric twice on the tacked lines, taking the point A towards the centre of the fabric until the diagonal lines falls on the outside fold line at B. Finger press across the diagonal line from edge to edge.

7 Open up the hem again and trim excess fabric diagonally to reduce any bulk.

8 Turn the hem under, folding the fabric on the fold lines to create the mitre at the corner. Tack the mitre and ladder stitch into position (see Fig. 25b on page 31).

9 Ladder stitch the angled sides together (Fig. 23c), starting from the inside edge and working to the tip of the corner, and then finish off by working a few stitches back towards the centre. This will not only strengthen the corner, but will give you the opportunity to get rid of any little bulges.
Secure the hem with hem stitch (see page 31) or pin stitch (see page 32).

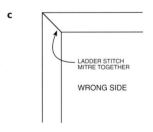

Withdrawing Threads for a Decorative Border or Hem

I To withdraw threads for a ladder hem stitch cut through the required number of horizontal threads to be withdrawn, 10 cm (4 in) from either side edge (Fig. 1). Carefully unravel the threads to the side edge, holding the fabric tightly at the sides to prevent the threads from pulling further than necessary.

Figs. 24a–b
Withdrawing threads for decorative border

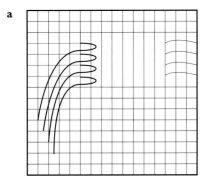

2 To secure, take the ends to the back of the fabric. Thread each end separately, follow the weave of the fabric and darn in the thread (Fig. 24b) for 1 cm (⅜ in) or stitch down with a small back stitch.

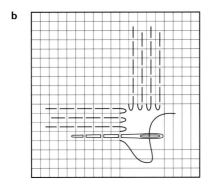

3 Withdraw the loose centre threads.

4 To form a corner, cut and withdraw the vertical threads in the same way as above (Fig. 24b).

Hem Stitch (Holsaum)

Hem stitching (Figs. 25a–c), a pulled thread technique, is a decorative way of securing a hem on evenweave fabric, or bordering garments and household linen. There are a number of different stitches used to secure a hem, all of which are equally acceptable, but only hem stitch and pin stitch are given in this book.

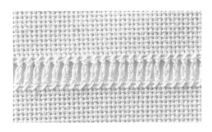

1 If hem stitch is being worked as a decorative line or border, it will just be worked through one thickness of fabric. If it is being worked to secure the hem, it will be stitched so that after a cluster of threads have been picked up, the needle comes through all three thicknesses of fabric turnings which make up the hem. Try to ensure that when you insert the needle (going through all the thicknesses of the hem) from the back of the work it is on the same level and is with the same number of threads as the front.

2 Stitch the hem, using the finer thread, from left to right and with the right or wrong side of the work facing you, depending on the effect you want. Bring the needle to the front two threads beneath the edge of the drawn threads at A or on the hem (Fig. 25a).

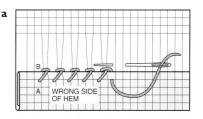

3 Take your thread across the front from left to right and pick up the first two vertical threads as shown. (Although two threads are shown and mentioned here, it could be three or four if more appropriate to the design.)

4 Wrap the threads and pull tightly, inserting the needle from the back to the front, and surfacing just to the right of the worked group of threads at B (Fig. 25b).

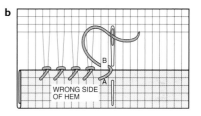

5 Repeat the stitch along the row, fastening off the thread as neatly as possible, travelling through the back of formed stitches and taking a small back stitch where possible.

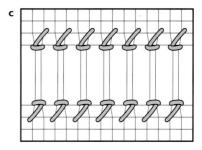

6 To work an opposite second row, turn the work around grouping the threads exactly opposite the first row and repeat the hem stitches as before. This is known as ladder hem stitch.

7 Working a ladder hem stitch will give you a casing for ribbon or cord.

Pin Stitch (Holfald)

This neat stitch (Figs. 26a–b) is another way of securing the hem with only a straight stitch showing on the front of the work. The working of the stitch causes little holes to appear along the hem beside the straight stitches, giving it a crisp, timeless quality.

I Prepare the hem in the usual way and, using the finer thread, bring your thread through the folds of the hem to the surface at A and with the wrong side facing you as shown (Fig. 26a).

Figs. 26a–b Pin stitch

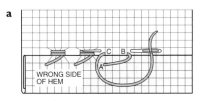

2 Insert the needle at B, picking up four threads (or two, if preferred) and coming out C.

3 Repeat this a second time so that the cluster of four threads is wrapped twice. Pull tightly.

4 Take the needle back to B and insert between the folded hem and the back of the fabric (so that no extra stitches other than the two wraps show on the right side) to come out at D.

5 Continue in this way until the row is finished.

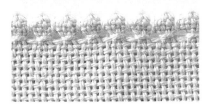

Back Stitch Picot with Open-sided Square Edging Stitch (Åpen Austmannarenningskant med tagger)

This combination stitch (Figs. 27a–d) is a wonderfully easy but impressive edging stitch. Three simple back stitches are worked in a horizontal line on the fold line edge, giving the effect of picots. The open-sided square edging stitch secures the hem and creates the open lacy effect.

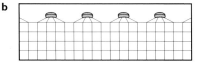

I The size of the 'picot' is determined by the thickness of thread. Use Coton Perlé No. 12 or similar for a fine picot and Coton Perlé No. 8 for a more prominent edge.

2 Leave at least 12 to 16 threads in from the edge (depending on the final depth of the edging you require) before withdrawing a single horizontal thread from your background fabric actually on the hem edge fold. You could always tack the outline to ensure that you do not pull out the wrong thread, but discard the tacking once you have pulled out the fabric thread. You will be sewing blocks of three back stitches along this line (Fig. 27a).

Figs. 27a–d Backstitch picot with open-sided square stitch

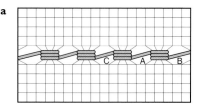

3 Come up through the fabric at A and take a back stitch over four threads to B.

4 Repeat AB twice more before progressing four more threads to surface at C. Make sure that all your back stitches lie side by side and are not 'stacked' up on top of each other.

5 Continue in this way until the outline is completed.

6 Bend over the hem and finger press so that the back stitch line is sitting 'proud' on the edge

(Fig.27b). Carefully mitre and stitch the corners.

7 Beads can be sewn in the hem so that they sit decoratively on the edge when the hem is folded over for working the open-sided square edging stitch. To work a beaded edge, a thread is withdrawn from the fabric as for back stitch picots.

8 With your beading needle and thread (doubled if the thread is fine) take a back stitch in the same manner as described above (see page 32) to bring the threads into a cluster. Bring the needle to the surface and thread on a bead. Make another back stitch. Pull tightly to position and 'settle' the bead on the surface before taking another back stitch through the bead and progressing to the next stitch. Repeat the process ensuring the beads are all facing in the same direction and sitting in position.

9 The open-sided square edging part of the stitch is worked through two thicknesses of the fabric to make a secure and decorative 'hem' edging. Start your first stitch a good 5 cm (2 in) away from a corner so that you can clearly see what you are doing. Work this part of the stitch

with the Coton Perlé No. 12 and bring the thread to the surface at A.

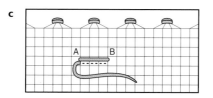

10 Take a back stitch over four threads to line up with the back stitch 'picots' and insert the needle at B (Fig.27c).

11 Pull firmly to create the holes and try not to distort the fabric. Repeat the process, but this time bring the needle across from behind the work to C (Fig.27d).

12 Take two back stitches from C to A and bring the needle back up at D. Repeat this process until the edging is completed, continuing round the mitred corners and keeping the stitches in line with the back stitch 'picots. The hem will be stronger if a second line of open-sided edging stitch is worked.

Double Picots with Open-sided Square Edging Stitch (Åpen Austmannarenningskant med tagger)

This is another excellent combination stitch (Figs. 28a–e) and a variation of the one above.

Groups of two Hedebo button-hole stitches are worked side by side in the withdrawn line on the hem fold to create 'picots'. This produces a much more prominent and fluted look to the hem edging.

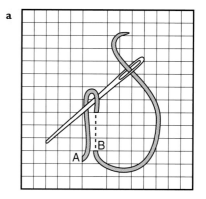

1 Refer to back stitch picot with open-sided square edging stitch, steps 1 and 2 (see page 32).

2 Work a pair of Hedebo buttonhole stitches coming to the surface at A (Fig. 28a), taking the sewing thread behind four fabric threads and out at B.

Figs. 28a–e Double picots with open-sided square edging

3 Insert the needle, from behind, through the top loop to make your first knot. Pull tightly upwards (Fig.28a).

b

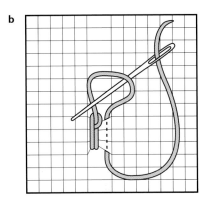

4 Repeat the process and carefully take your thread to the back behind the buttonhole stitches to emerge at C (Fig.28c). The buttonhole stitches will be slightly pulled to one side as the thread is taken behind, but will stand out like small knots once the edge is folded.

c

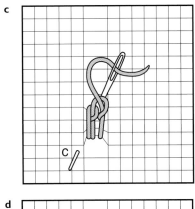

d

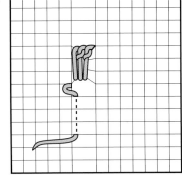

5 Hook the thread round one fabric thread before going down behind the subsequent four

threads (Fig.28d) to start the next buttonhole stitch. Repeat the process until the outline is completed.

e

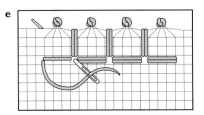

6 To finish the hem edging, refer to back stitch picot with open-sided square edging stitch, steps 6–12 (see page 32–3).

7 More rows may be worked if a deeper lacy edge is required, but remember to make allowance for this when you plan where to start your hem.

Four-sided Stitch (Austmannarenning)

This decorative pulled thread stitch (Figs. 29a–d) can be used as border or filling stitch. It can be worked over two, three or four threads and is particularly effective when used with dense surface embroidery acting as a contrast in texture.

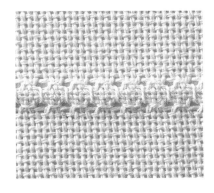

1 Use the finer thread and work from right to left.

2 Bring the thread to the surface at A and insert the needle at B, four (or two) threads above A. Pull firmly, but not enough to distort the fabric.

Figs. 29a–d Four-sided stitch (square stitch)

a

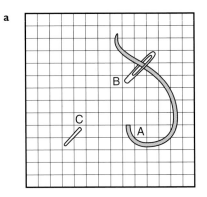

3 Come out at C. Insert the thread at A again and come back out at D (Fig.29b).

b

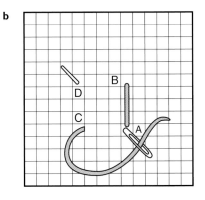

4 Take the needle back down at B and surface at C to continue in this way to the end of the row. Pull all the stitches firmly as you work each one (Fig.29c).

c

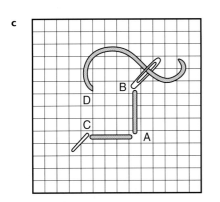

d

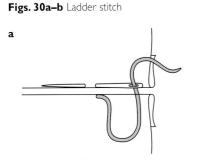

Ladder Stitch

This invaluable stitch (Figs. 30a–b) gives you invisible seam joins.

1 Butt the two edges to be joined.

2 Secure the thread and take the needle from one edge and insert it in the other edge directly opposite.

Figs. 30a–b Ladder stitch

a

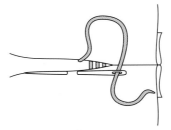

3 Take a small horizontal stitch and repeat the process.

4 Work four small horizontal stitches before pulling up the

thread to bring the edges close together.

b

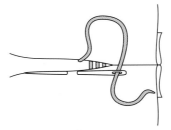

FINISHING-OFF TECHNIQUES

Sewing on a Bead

1 Bring a fine or beading needle to the front of the fabric, thread on a bead and take a small stitch back into the fabric.

2 If you a have a lot of single beads to sew on, make several small back stitches after every third bead to secure.

Making a Buttonholed Ring

1 Cut a length of thread at least 1.35 m (1½ yd) long using Coton Perlé No. 8 (the finer the thread the more you will need).

2 Tie one end of the thread to the ring (as shown) and attach your needle to the other end (Fig. 31a).

Figs. 31a–b Buttonhole a ring to hang ribbons on

a

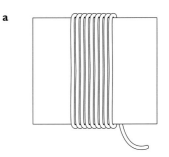

3 Keeping the stitches close together, work buttonhole stitch all round the ring in a clockwise direction. As you get close to the beginning, undo the knot and bind in the loose end with about the last twelve stitches. Finish off the thread by taking the needle and thread through the stitches already worked. Turn the buttonhole edge to the inside (Fig. 31b).

b

Making a Simple Tassel

Used singly or grouped, tassels are an excellent and exotic finishing touch. They can be attached as a specific detail, grouped for effect and added just for fun. Use fibres which hang well, and do not be afraid to mix colours and textures of yarns. Different thicknesses produce alternative effects.

1 Wind the required number of threads round a piece of card which you have cut to the length of the tassel needed (Fig. 32a).

Figs. 32a–c Simple Tassel

a

2 Gather up the top of the loops on to a cord or length of threads. Slide the card through the loops or cut through the bottom of the loops to release (Fig. 32b).

b

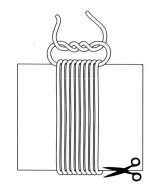

3 Bind the tassel about 12 mm (½ in) from the top with a needle and thread, or wrap.

4 To wrap, make a loop in the thread and position this lying on top of the tassel threads. Take the wrapping thread tightly around the tassel five or six times. Finish off by threading the end through the loop (Fig. 32c).

c

5 Pull the loop up tightly to take the opposite end underneath the wrap. Trim the tails close to the wrapping.

6 Trim the tassel ends and, if necessary, steam gently over water to 'fluff out' the fibres.

Making a Basic Twisted Cord

Twisted cords can be made from many different types of thread, to any thickness you like.

1 If you are going to mix your threads, choose them carefully because not all threads twist in the same manner.

2 Cut the number of threads, three times the required finished length.

3 Knot each end to form a loop, and insert a pencil (Fig. 33a).

Figs. 33a–c How to make a cord (stage 1)

a

4 Twist the pencil keeping the threads taut (Fig. 33b).

b

5 When the cord looks tight enough to twist back on itself bring the pencil to meet the hook, holding the centre point firmly (Fig. 33c).

c

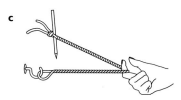

6 Allow the cord to twist together a little at a time.

7 Knot or wrap the ends with thread to secure.

Sewing on a Cord

1 Stitch the cord in place round the edges of the project (Fig. 34), working a slanting stitch following the twist of the cord.

Fig. 34 How to sew on a cord

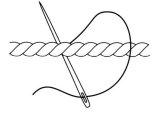

2 The joining of the cord or finishing off depends on the finished look of each particular project. It will either be tucked down and hidden by the side seam or hidden behind a knot and is described with each project.

Lacing Your Embroidery

1 If applicable, wash the embroidery before lacing.

2 Use a piece of cardboard that has been cut to the required size. Acid-free card is available from art shops or picture framers.

3 Tack the finished size of the embroidery on your fabric, following the straight grain of the fabric.

4 Place the embroidery right side down on a clean surface and line

up the card on the tacked outline on the back.

5 Position with pins inserted into the edge of the card.

6 Using a length of strong thread sufficient to complete a side, lace across the back, working from the centre outwards (Fig.35). Pull the thread tightly. Complete the other side.

Fig.35 Lacing on a card

7 Repeat in the other direction, lacing under and over the first line of threads, again working from the centre to the sides.

8 Check continuously that the front is still straight, adjusting if necessary.

9 Fold over the corners and complete the lacing right to the edges.

10 Cover the lacing with a piece of fabric hemmed into position.

INTRODUCING HARDANGER DESIGNS

PRACTICE SAMPLER 1

The stitches for this sampler are shown on pages 17–23.

Finished size: 9 cm (3½ in) square

Materials

19 cm (7½ in) square Zweigart Lugana, 25 threads to the inch, colour No. 535 sky

1 ball of DMC Coton Perlé No. 8 white

1 ball of DMC Coton Perlé No. 12 white

Method

1 Refer to the techniques and stitches sections on pages 15–37. Prepare your linen as described and tack in central lines in both directions.

2 Using the white Coton Perlé No. 8, follow the chart and begin working the kloster blocks. Start your first stitch at A, 30 threads down from the centre point and two threads to the right of the vertical centre line.

3 Stitch the kloster blocks forming the central diamond shape as shown by the broken line, followed by the straight lines forming the inner and outer outlining squares. Fill in the extra kloster blocks in the corner.

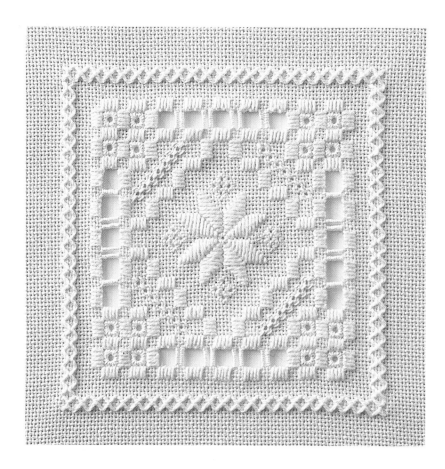

4 Still using Coton Perlé No. 8, complete the central star and twisted lattice band border. Make sure the stitches of the twisted lattice band are in line with the kloster blocks.

5 With Coton Perlé No. 12, work all the square and diagonal eyelets. When working the central eyelet you will find the stitches from the star slightly cover the holes you need. Gently push them away so that you go into the right place.

6 Complete the reversed diagonal faggoting.

7 Cut and withdraw threads in the middle of the design as shown on the chart.

8 If it is more comfortable, turn the work when necessary to stitch the woven or wrapped bars.

9 Needleweave or wrap the bars with Coton Perlé No. 12, starting at B. Complete all four sides of the design as shown in the chart. Wash and press the work (see page 17). Make up the completed design as you wish.

KEY

Stitch/Thread

 Kloster blocks
DMC Coton Perlé No. 8

Satin stitch star
DMC Coton Perlé No. 8

Twisted lattice band
DMC Coton Perlé No. 8

Square and diagonal eyelets
DMC Coton Perlé No. 12

 Reversed diagonal faggoting
DMC Coton Perlé No. 12

Needleweaving
DMC Coton Perlé No. 12

Cut threads

Wrapped bars
DMC Coton Perlé No. 12

PRACTICE SAMPLER 2

The stitches for this sampler are
shown on pages 17–26.
Finished size: 9 cm (3½ in) square

Materials
19 cm (7½ in) Zweigart Lugana, 25
  threads to the inch, colour No.
  535 sky
1 ball of DMC Coton Perlé No. 8
  white
1 ball of DMC Coton Perlé No. 12
  white

Method

1 Refer to the techniques and stitches
  sections on pages 15–37. Prepare
  your linen as described and tack in
  central lines in both directions.

2 Using the white Coton Perlé No. 8,
  follow the chart and begin working
  the kloster blocks. Start your first
  stitch at A, 14 threads down from
  the centre point and two threads to
  the right of the vertical centre line.

3 Stitch the kloster blocks forming
  the central diamond shape as
  shown by the broken line (in the
  outer diamond shape), followed by
  the blocks forming the outer
  diamond shape starting at B. Work
  the straight lines forming the inner
  and outer outlining squares. Lastly
  fill in the extra kloster blocks
  squeezed between the two outlines.
  Do these last because you can then
  move back and forth from each
  block through the blocks already
  established on the side.

4 Still using Coton Perlé No. 8,
  complete the twisted lattice band.

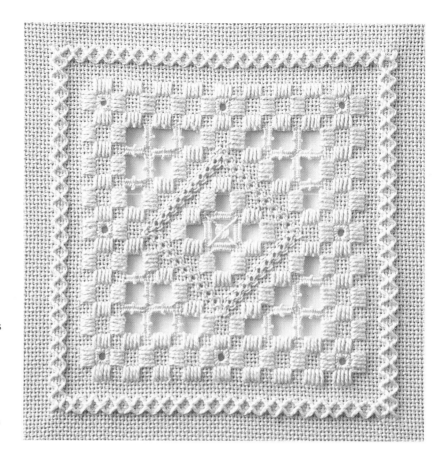

Make sure the stitches of the
twisted lattice band are in line
with the kloster blocks.

5 With Coton Perlé No. 12, stitch all
  the eyelets and reversed diagonal
  faggoting.

6 Cut and withdraw the threads as
  shown on the chart. Cut one side
  section at a time so you do not
  distort the fabric whilst you are
  sewing another side.

7 Following the directional arrows,
  start needleweaving the bars at C
  using Coton Perlé No. 12. When
  you reach the centre of the bar,
  put a picot knot on each side
  before completing the rest of the
  bar. Having worked a complete

diagonal line, finish off the thread
and start again at D to finish
weaving the final bars. If you
prefer the bars may simply be
woven. Complete all four corners
in this manner.

8 In the centre design there is a
  spider's web filling, but you may
  prefer to use picot knots or a
  dove's eye as a filling. Start
  needleweaving the bar at E and
  include the filling of your choice,
  referring to the instructions earlier
  in this chapter.

9 Wash and press the work (see page
  17). Make up the completed
  design as you wish.

KEY

Stitch/Thread

 Kloster blocks
DMC Coton Perlé No. 8

Square eyelets
DMC Coton Perlé No. 12

 Reversed diagonal faggoting
DMC Coton Perlé No. 12

 Twisted lattice band
DMC Coton Perlé No. 8

Needleweaving and picot knots
DMC Coton Perlé No. 12

 Needleweaving and spider's
web filling
DMC Coton Perlé No. 12

PRACTICE SAMPLER 3

The stitches for this sampler are
shown on pages 17–28.
Finished size: 10 cm (4 in) across

Materials

25 cm (10 in) square Zweigart
Lugana, 25 threads to the inch,
colour No. 535 sky
1 ball of DMC Coton Perlé No.
8 white
1 ball of DMC Coton Perlé No. 12
white

Method

1 Refer to the techniques and
stitches sections on pages 15–37.
Prepare your linen as described
and tack in central lines in both
directions.

2 Using the white Coton Perlé No.
8, follow the chart and begin
working the kloster blocks. Start
your first stitch at A, 30 threads
down from the centre point and
two threads to the right of the
vertical centre line.

3 Stitch the kloster blocks forming
the central diamond shape as
shown by the broken line. Work
the kloster blocks forming the
outer diamond shape starting at
B. The small isolated square of
kloster blocks in the middle has
to stand on its own with all the
threads starting and finishing in
the one shape.

4 Outline the whole design as
shown in the chart with
buttonhole stitch.

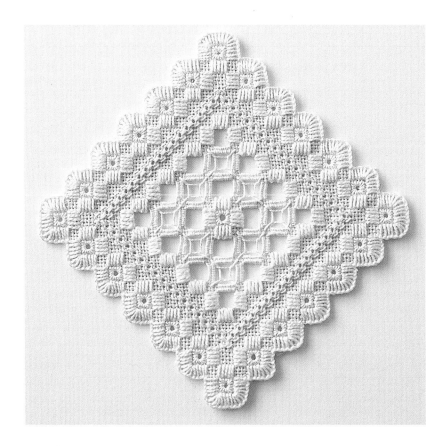

5 Change to the Coton Perlé No.
12 and work the reversed
diagonal faggoting and all the
eyelets. Be methodical and work
round the whole design in
sequence, one eyelet after another.

6 Cut and withdraw the threads
from the centre shape as shown
on the chart.

7 Following the directional arrows,
needleweave the bars with Coton
Perlé No. 12 starting at C.
Combine the woven bars with a
filling of your choice. The filet

filling has been worked on this
sample and is shown on the chart,
but you can change this to suit
yourself, referring to the
instructions earlier in this chapter.

8 Carefully wash and press the
embroidery (see page 17) before
cutting the design away from the
background. Refer to the section
on cutting away from the
buttonhole stitches (see page 27)
before you start.

9 If you made two of these to
match, they could be sewn
together and filled with pot-
pourri. Sew on a loop and tassel
to turn it into a small hanging.

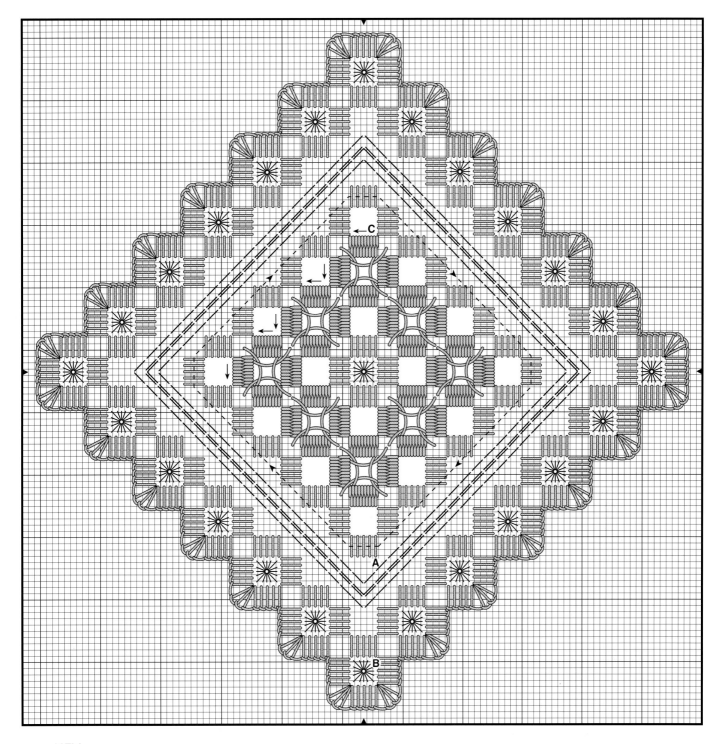

KEY   **Stitch/Thread**

    Kloster blocks
DMC Coton Perlé No. 8

   Buttonhole edging
DMC Coton Perlé No. 8

    Square eyelets
DMC Coton Perlé No. 12

    Reversed diagonal faggoting
DMC Coton Perlé No. 12

    Needleweaving and square
filet filling
DMC Coton Perlé No. 12

CHAPTER 2

LABOURS OF LOVE

NO APOLOGY IS NEEDED FOR 'LABOURS OF LOVE' IN

HARDANGER EMBROIDERY. ANY OF THE PROJECTS IN THIS

CHAPTER WOULD MAKE A LASTING AND TREASURED

MEMENTO FOR A SPECIAL OCCASION TO GIVE TO A FRIEND

OR MEMBER OF YOUR FAMILY.

- Ribbon, beads and metallic thread gleam and glisten with Hardanger stitches to create a traditional white sampler with contemporary appeal.

- White for a prayer book or practical blue and multicoloured threads for every day make the bookmark a versatile choice.

- A heart pomander hanging in white and red could be made for a touch of romance.

- Simple white or multicoloured thread and pastel linen combine to make a lavender bag to treasure and enjoy.

- A pincushion in rich wine red with an interesting beaded edging is not only practical, but decorative.

- A small scissors keeper in bright colours, with beads and tassels, will ensure your scissors are always easy to find.

- A photograph frame with a delicate heart design in white will border any of your favourite pictures.

HARDANGER SAMPLER

This sampler is based on the traditional long and narrow band sampler typical of the seventeenth century which showed border patterns to be used on linen or clothing. Design bands were often placed close together at this time. The bands of this modern version develop from the simple to the more complicated, giving scope to practise Hardanger stitches as well as becoming an exquisite decorative panel to treasure.

There is much scope in this design for experimenting with your own colour schemes, using shaded or space dyed threads, and introducing more metallic threads such as Kreinik metallics, blending filament, very fine and fine braids or DMC Fil or Clair to work the stitches.

Simple bands of stitches make effective borders for larger projects, such as a strip border for a place mat or tray cloth.

Finished size: 25 x 14 cm (10 x 5½ in)

Materials
- 35.5 x 24 cm (14 x 9½ in) Zweigart Lugana, 25 threads to the inch, colour white
- 1 ball of DMC Coton Perlé No. 8 white
- 1 ball of DMC Coton Perlé No. 12 white
- Kreinik blending filament silver 001
- 29 x 16.5 cm (11½ x 6½ in) coloured acid-free mounting board
- 1 m (1¼ yd) satin ribbon (white or colour of choice)
- 300 iridescent beads (white or colour of choice to match ribbon)

Method
1 Refer to the techniques section on pages 17–37. Prepare your linen as described and tack in the vertical centre line.

2 Using the Coton Perlé No. 8, start your first line of stitching at A, 5 cm (2 in) in from the top and the right-hand side edge.

3 Work from the top to the bottom of the sampler. Stitch the bands following the chart and key. Work to the centre and repeat for the other half of the design. Make a point of checking that the kloster blocks are exactly lined up, that you start on the correct thread at the beginning of each line.

4 The stitches and fillings in the sampler will be found in projects throughout the book.

5 For the bands of four-sided stitch (bands 2, 4, 16 and 18 on the chart), use a shorter thread and combine the Kreinik blending filament in your needle with the Coton Perlé No. 12.

6 After completing all the bands, thread the satin ribbon through the casing formed by the hem stitching. Sew on the beads (see page 35) using a back stitch.

7 Carefully wash and press the embroidery, keeping the lines as straight as possible. Lace the embroidery (see page 36–7) on to the coloured acid-free board before taking it to be framed by a professional framer or making it up as you wish.

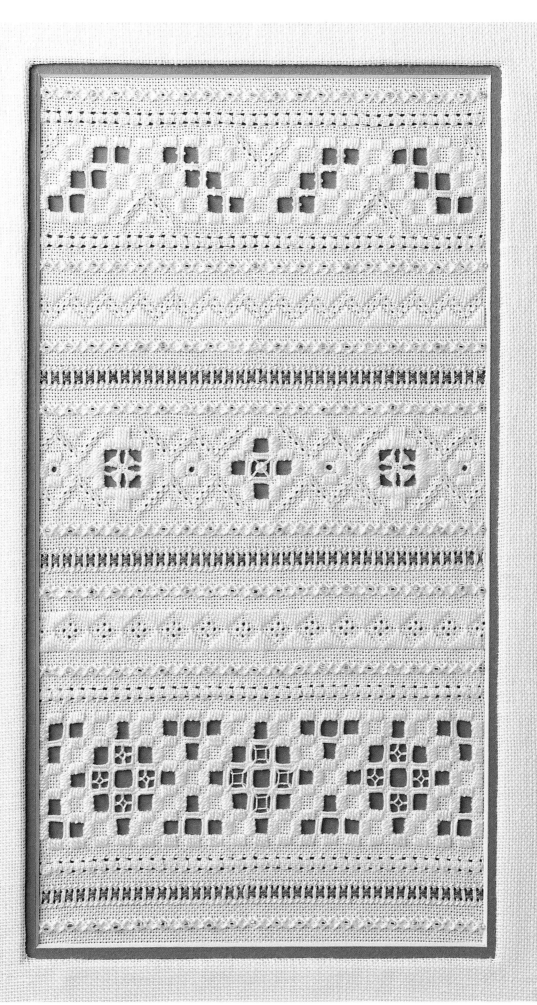

KEY

	Band No.	Stitch/Thread
	1, 5, 7, 9, 11, 13, 15, 20	Twisted lattice band (bead in centreoptional) Coton Perlé No. 8
	8, 12, 19	Hem stitch (4 threads apart) Coton Perlé No. 12
	3, 10, 17	Kloster blocks Coton Perlé No. 8
	3, 6, 10	Reversed diagonal faggoting Coton Perlé No. 12
	10	Square eyelets Coton Perlé No. 12
	2, 4, 16, 18	Four-sided stitch Coton Perlé No.12, Kreinik blending filament 001
	3	Needleweaving with picot knots Coton Perlé No. 12
	6	Satin stitch with reversed diagonal faggoting Coton Perlé No. 8
	3, 10	Satin stitch pyramids Coton Perlé No. 8
	10	Greek cross filling Coton Perlé No. 12
	10	Needleweaving with spider's web filling Coton Perlé No. 12
	14	Satin stitches with diagonal eyelets Coton Perlé No. 12
	17	Needleweaving with dove's eye filling Coton Perlé No. 12
	17	Needleweaving with square filet filling Coton Perlé No. 12

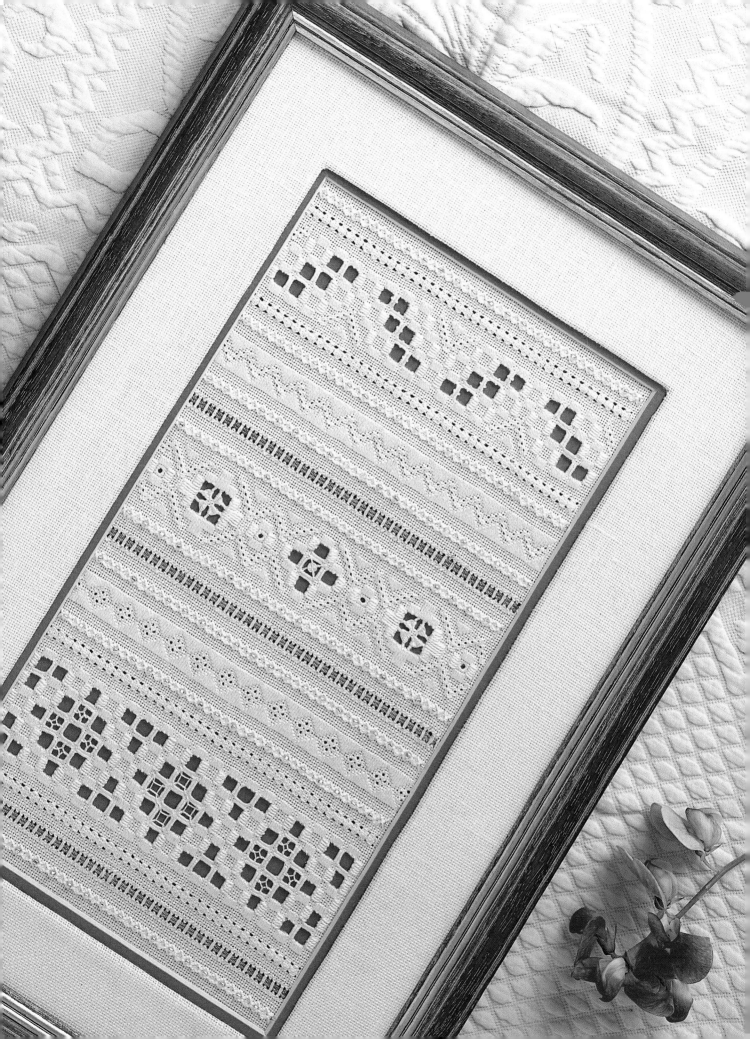

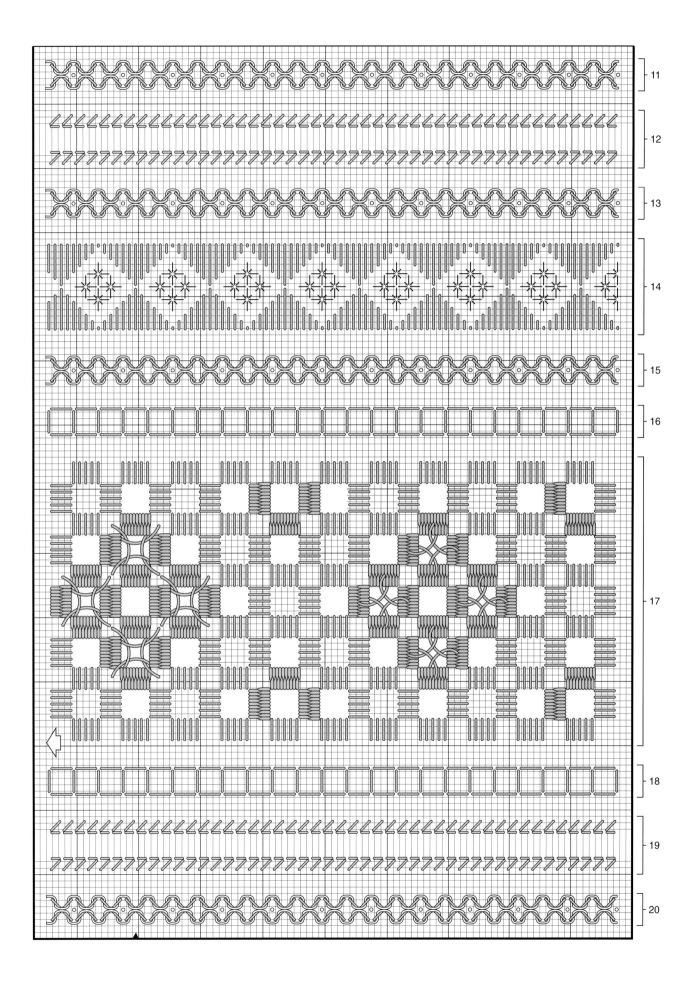

BOOKMARK

Bookmarks are small, but very personal. With its distinctive 'fluted' edge and simple design of basic Hardanger stitches, this is a bookmark to admire and make for a friend. With this simple design of basic Hardanger stitches, you could make a whole collection if you wished and, for the adventurous, the four small traditional diamond shapes give you the freedom to try a variety of filling stitches.

Finished size: 16.5 x 5 cm (6½ x 2 in)

Materials

White Version

- 23 cm (9 in) square Minster linen, 28 threads to the inch, colour white
- 1 ball of DMC Coton Perlé No. 8 white
- 1 ball of DMC Coton Perlé No. 12 white

Blue Version

- 23 cm (9 in) square Jobelan evenweave, 28 threads to the inch, colour No. 01 dark blue
- 1 ball of DMC Coton Perlé No. 8 colour No. 797
- 1 skein Caron Collection Wildflowers, colour Nefertiti

Method

1 Refer to the techniques section on pages 17–37. Prepare your fabric as described. (The generous fabric allowance makes the small design easier to handle and sew.)

2 Following the chart and using Coton Perlé No. 8, start the kloster blocks with your first stitch at A, 5.5 cm (2¼ in) up from the bottom edge and 8 cm (3¼ in) in from the right-hand edge.

3 Work up the long diagonal line of kloster blocks to form the outline rectangle of the bookmark. At this stage, run a diagonal tacking line the entire length of the bookmark, as shown on the chart. It will help you to find the centre point of the square eyelets and check your positioning.

4 Complete the kloster blocks for all the inner small diamond shapes and fill in the extra blocks at the end. If you prefer to have both ends pointed, follow the chart and reverse the fill in of extra blocks. Equally, if you prefer straight ends, do not work the extra blocks.

5 Stitch the buttonhole edging round the entire design.

6 Fill in all the eyelets using Coton Perlé No. 12 (or the equivalent) and work the reversed diagonal faggoting.

7 Cut and withdraw the threads in the small diamonds and, continuing with Coton Perlé No. 12 (or the equivalent), needleweave the bars starting at B. These can either be done simply, with picot knots or looped picots, or with other fillings, such as the dove's eye, spider's web, or square filet.

8 Carefully wash and press the embroidery (see page 17) before cutting the design away from the background. Refer to the section on cutting away from the buttonhole stitches (see page 27) before you start and remember always to cut from the back of the work.

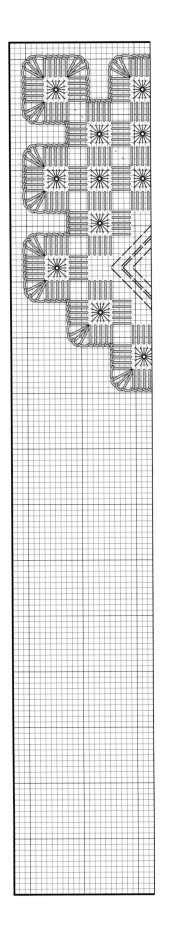

KEY

Stitch/Thread

(blue version in brackets)

Kloster blocks

DMC Coton Perlé No. 8, white

Buttonhole edging

DMC Coton Perlé No. 8, white

(DMC Coton Perlé No. 8, Colour 797)

Reversed diagonal faggoting

DMC Coton Perlé No. 12, white (2 strands DMC Stranded

Cotton, Colour No. 797)

Square eyelets

DMC Coton Perlé No. 12, white (Caron Collection

Watercolours, Colour Nefertiti)

Needleweaving

DMC Coton Perlé No. 12, white (Caron Collection

Watercolours, Colour Nefertiti)

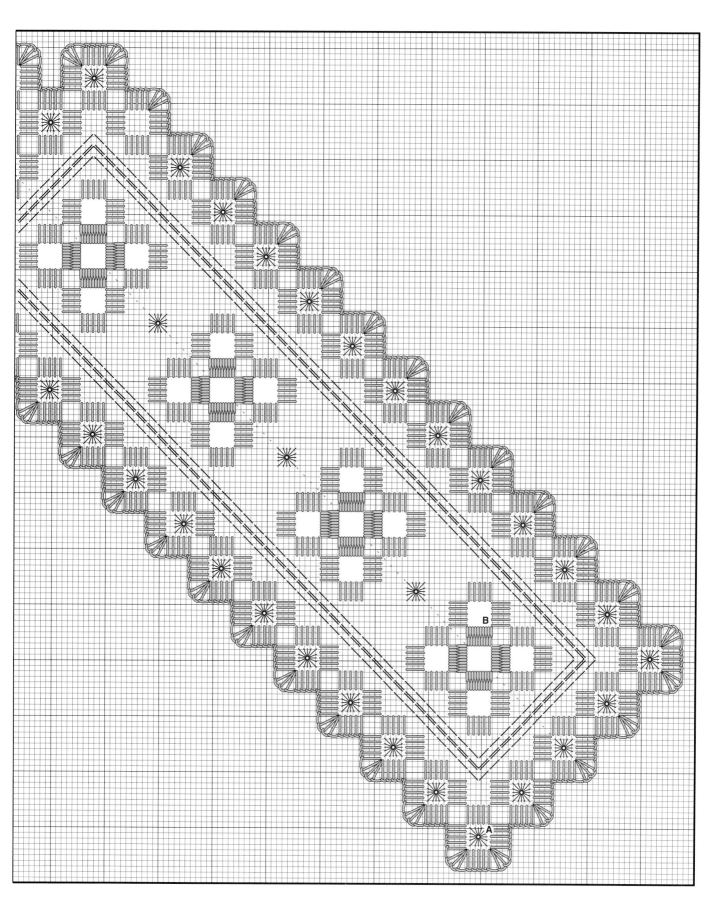

HEART POMANDER

Historically, pomanders were a ball made of sweet-smelling herbs, worn on neck chains and girdles or carried. Sometimes the pomanders had several different partitions, each containing a different scent.

Filled with fragrant oils, hearts hanging attractively as a mobile or just singly as a small wall decoration are a contemporary interpretation of this traditional item. Choose pure whites for your bedroom or vibrant reds for a Valentine. Fillings of knots, looped picots or dove's eyes add delicacy to the shape.

Finished size: 5 x 3.8 cm (2 x 1½ in)

Materials

(for each heart, front and back)

- 15 x 20.5 cm (6 x 8 in) Minster linen, 28 threads to the inch, colour white
- 1 ball of DMC Coton Perlé No. 8 white
- 1 ball of DMC Coton Perlé No. 12 white
- 12.5 x 18 cm (5 x 7 in) contrasting or matching lining for the hearts

- Small white cottonwool ball
- A few drops of fragrant environmental oil
- Small plastic envelope or cling film
- 68.5 cm (27 in) cord or ribbon for hanging

Method

1 Refer to the techniques section on pages 17–37. Prepare your linen as described and tack in the centre vertical line. (The generous fabric allowance makes the small design easier to handle and sew.)

2 Using Coton Perlé No. 8, start the kloster blocks with your first stitch at A, 5 cm (2 in) up from the bottom edge and two threads to the right of the vertical centre line.

3 Work the kloster blocks round the inner heart shape, referring to the chart.

4 Complete the buttonhole edging.

5 Changing to the Coton Perlé No. 12, stitch all the eyelets.

6 Cut and withdraw the threads to work the needleweaving, starting at B, and using a filling of your choice. Dove's eye filling is shown on the chart. On the three-heart mobile the fillings are different in each heart. The top one is needlewoven with picot knots, the second with a dove's eye filling and the third incorporates both the picot knots and dove's eye filling.

7 Make a second heart for the back, starting 12 mm (½ in) above the first heart. (If you are short of time, you could just work the outline kloster blocks, buttonhole hole edging and eyelets.)

8 Carefully wash and press the embroidery (see page 17) before cutting the design away from the background. Refer to the section on cutting away from the buttonhole stitches before you start (see page 27).

9 To line the hearts, cut two pieces of the lining fabric to the shape of the hearts. Slip stitch into place on the back of each heart to cover all the open work. Make sure no pieces of fabric are sticking up from behind. You can use fray check on the raw edges as it is not necessary to turn in a hem.

10 Put a few drops of your oil on to the cottonwool and place in the plastic pocket (cutting off the top so that it is open) or wrap in cling film leaving an opening at the top for the fragrance to escape into the room and so that the pomander may be refreshed when necessary.

11 Cut the cord or ribbon into three lengths: 16.5 cm (6½ in), 22 cm (8½ in) and 30 cm (12 in) and attach to a buttonhole ring (see page 35). To attach cords or ribbons to the buttonholed ring, fold the ends over the ring and wrap into position (see page 36). Bind the opposite end before stitching each ribbon or cord to the inside of one heart shape. Add beads or tassels (see pages 35–36) as preferred.

12 Place the hearts together, back to back and sandwiching the scented filling. Carefully overstitch together on the buttonhole edging. Leave a small opening at the top of the heart shape so that you can change or refresh your filling when necessary.

KEY

Stitch/Thread

Kloster blocks
DMC Coton Perlé No. 8, white

Buttonhole edging
DMC Coton Perlé No. 8, white

Square eyelets
DMC Coton Perlé No. 12, white

Needleweaving with dove's eye
DMC Coton Perlé No. 12, white

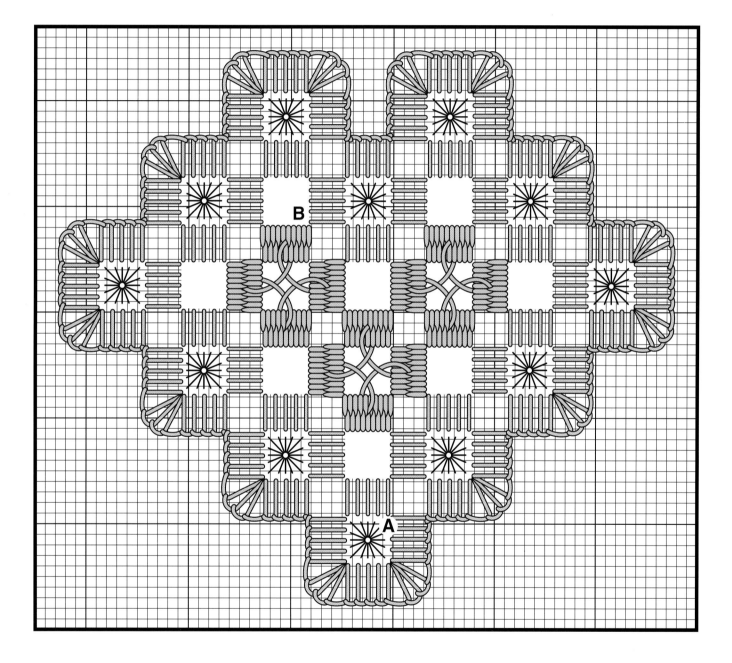

LAVENDER BAG

Fill this small sachet with fragrant lavender and savour the fresh, all-pervading scent in your cupboards and drawers – or hang it on the wall to enjoy the aroma and appreciate the Hardanger embroidery. The simple design follows the shape of the bag, and small beads or pearls add a delicate lustre to the linen. Alternatively you could decorate the surrounds with small stems of lavender worked in delicate French knots or fly stitch.

Finished size of bag: 10 x 18 cm (4 x 7 in)
Finished size of sachet: 9 x 12.5 cm (3½ x 5 in)

Materials

Lilac Lavender Bag
- 15 x 40.5 cm (6 x 16 in) Zweigart Brittney linen, 28 threads to the inch, colour No. 559 lilac
- Oliver Twist hand-dyed Hardanger skeins of pinks and mauves or similar (two weights)
- Pearl beads (optional)
- 1 m (1¼ yd) matching or contrasting satin ribbon, 2–3 mm (¹⁄₁₆–⅛ in) wide ribbon or hand-made cord, for drawstring
- Beading needle and thread, for attaching beads
- 20.5 x 28 cm (8 x 11 in) contrasting cotton fabric, to make lavender sachet
- Dried lavender

White Version (fabric and threads)
- 15 x 40.5 cm (6 x 16 in) Minster linen, 28 threads to the inch, colour white
- 1 ball of DMC Coton Perlé No. 8 white
- 1 ball of DMC Coton Perlé No. 12 white

Method

1 Refer to the techniques section on pages 17–37. Prepare your linen as described.

2 Tack in the centre line in both directions on your piece of fabric. The fabric will be folded in half horizontally to make the bag and the design may be worked on one or both sides.

3 Using the white Coton Perlé No. 8, follow the chart and work the kloster blocks, starting your first stitch at A, 18 mm (¾ in) or 22 threads up from the centre fold and two threads to the right of the vertical centre line.

4 Work the lozenge shape of kloster blocks, followed by the inner diamond shape and lastly the outlining kloster blocks.

5 Complete the central star motif still using the Coton Perlé No. 8.

6 Change your thread to the Coton Perlé No. 12 to stitch the reversed diagonal faggoting, the four square eyelets round the star motif and all the square eyelets at the top of the design.

7 Cut and withdraw the threads and using Coton Perlé No. 12 start the needleweaving at B. Complete one half of the design before reversing the procedure to complete the other side.

8 Needleweave the three single bars following the directional arrows, and finishing off in the back of a kloster block with a back stitch so that as you move to the next bar the previous one is not pulled out of line.

9 With a new thread begin needleweaving the more open area starting at C and working diagonally, as shown by the directional arrows. Return to the top of the next diagonal line D and complete as before, finally finishing off the last two bars in the right-hand corner.

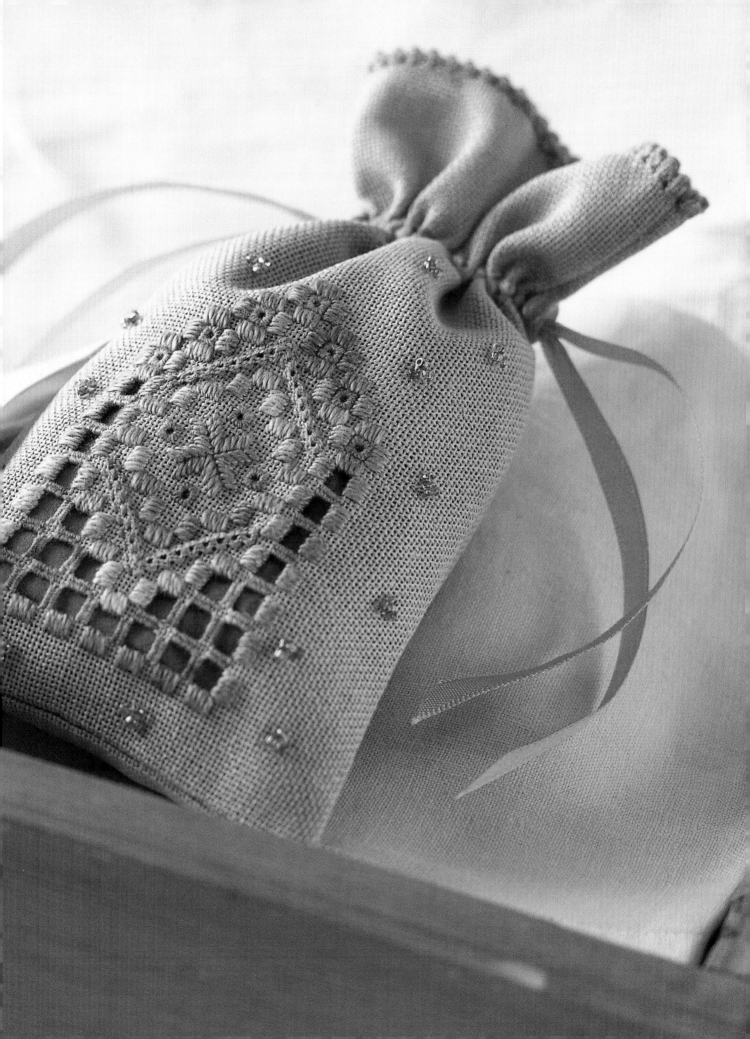

10 Repeat the whole design on the other side of the central fold line, remembering to turn the fabric so that you work the design the same way as before starting at E.

11 Counting 28 threads (2.5 cm/1 in) from the side edge of the design, stitch a line of tacking the entire length of the fabric (on either side) to mark the edge of the bag.

12 For the casing measure 3.5 cm (1⅜ in) from the top of the design and, starting in the middle, cut up through the next six threads (running horizontally across the work and withdraw). Prepare for hem stitching as instructed on page 30. Repeat exactly on the other side of the bag.

13 Hem stitch on both sides of the casing using Coton Perlé No. 12, remembering to ensure your stitches are in line with the kloster blocks. Turn the work to execute the opposite line of hem stitching. Repeat on other side of the bag.

14 Wash and press the work (see page 17).

15 Randomly sew on pearls, singly, or clustered, if wished, before sewing up the side seams.

16 With the fabric folded in half at the tacked centre line, right sides together, tack and then sew or machine up the entire length of the side seams. Use the original tacking lines as a guide to keep the seams straight. Trim off excess fabric from the side seams to 6 mm (¼ in), press open and oversew or machine zigzag to prevent fraying. Turn inside out and press.

17 On the right side, measure 3.5 cm (1⅜ in) from the top row of hem stitching forming the casing (on both sides of the bag) and pull out the next thread (horizontally across the work) ready for working the decorative edging stitch.

18 In this withdrawn line, work the first part of the back stitch picot edging (see page 32) using Coton Perlé No. 8. Fold over the edge to the inside and stitch one row of open-sided square stitch using Coton Perlé No.

12. Trim off the excess fabric close to the stitching.

19 Thread ribbons or cord through the casing as you wish. To achieve double drawstrings, thread one length of ribbon or cord from one side seam, right the way round through the casing and returning to the start. Then thread the other length in the same manner starting from the opposite side seam. Pull up and finish off both ends with either a knot, bead or tassel.

20 Using the contrasting cotton to show up the Hardanger, make a small sachet 9 x 12.5 cm (3½ x 5 in) and fill with lavender.

21 Place the sachet in the bag and pull up the drawstrings to complete the project.

KEY

	Stitch/Thread
	Kloster blocks DMC Coton Perlé No. 8
	Simple star DMC Coton Perlé No. 8
	Square eyelets DMC Coton Perlé No. 12
	Reversed diagonal faggoting DMC Coton Perlé No. 12
	Needleweaving DMC Coton Perlé No. 12
	Back stitch picot and open sided square stitch DMC Coton Perlé No. 12
	Hem stitch (casing) DMC Coton Perlé No. 12

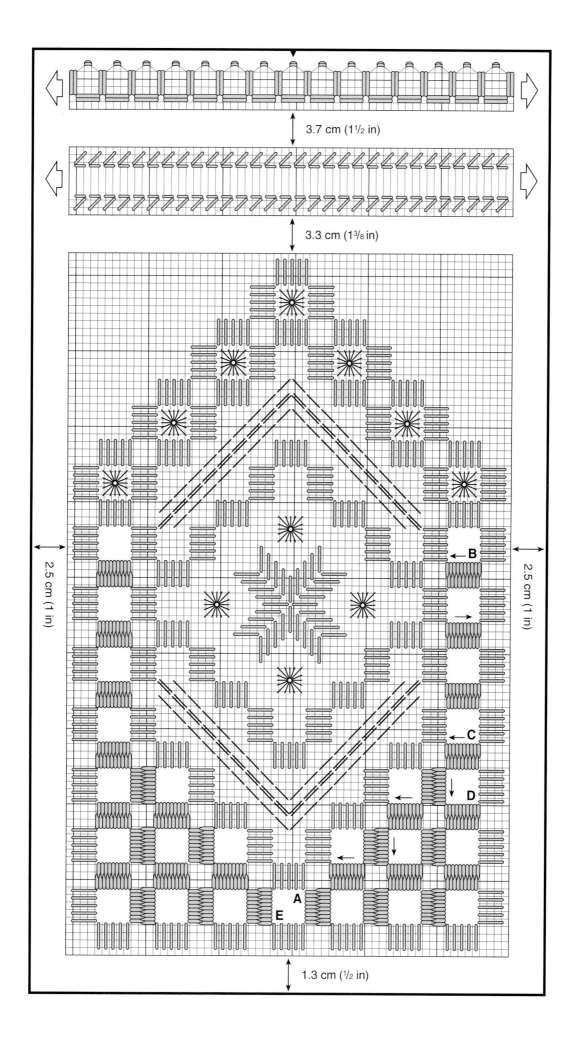

3.7 cm (1½ in)

3.3 cm (1⅜ in)

2.5 cm (1 in)

2.5 cm (1 in)

B

C

D

A

E

1.3 cm (½ in)

PINCUSHION

Show off your pins and needles on this practical wine-coloured pincushion alluringly edged with matching beads. A central motif of Greek cross filling is surrounded by kloster blocks and the design for needleweaving is cut in a way often seen and worked on traditional pieces. Beads could be added to the lattice band border to echo the edging and outline the design.

Finished size: 12 cm (4¾ in) square

Materials

- 22.5 cm (8¾ in) square Zweigart Brittney linen, 28 threads to the inch, colour No. 906
- 1 ball of DMC Coton Perlé No. 8 colour No. 816
- 1 skein DMC stranded cotton colour No. 816 (or Caron Collection Wildflowers colour flame)
- 22.5 cm (8¾ in) cotton contrasting fabric to line embroidery
- 22.5 cm (8¾ in) backing fabric and thread to match for pincushion

- Small packet seed beads, size 11 (optional)
- Beading needle and thread to match project
- Preferred pincushion filling (or see instructions on page 68)

Method

1 Refer to the techniques section on pages 17–37. Prepare your linen as described and tack in the central horizontal and vertical lines.

2 Following the chart and using Coton Perlé No. 8, work the kloster block outline starting your first stitch at A, 30 threads down from the centre point and two threads to the right of the vertical centre line.

3 Stitch the next shape, starting at B, followed by the outlining square of blocks.

4 Fill in the remaining diagonal lines of kloster blocks, the corner and central motifs and twisted lattice band.

5 Using two strands of DMC stranded cotton No. 816, work the eyelets and reversed diagonal faggoting .

6 Cut and withdraw the threads, referring to the chart. Needleweave the central motif and combine with a Greek cross filling. Knots, looped picots or twisted bars could be used as an alternative. (Do not worry if you make a mistake with the cutting; simply cut the whole shape as shown in Sampler 3 (see page 42) and needleweave with a filling of your choice.)

7 Needleweave the main design as shown, starting at C and following the directional arrows.

8 To make the beaded edge, follow the method described on page 33, but in this instance do not pull a fabric thread. Start your first back stitch in the middle of a straight edge eight threads away from the lattice band. Remember to mitre the corners (see page 30).

9 Finger press the fold so that the beads are sitting upright on the edge. Secure the hem with the one row of open-sided square edging stitch using Coton Perlé No. 8 colour No. 816. Do not trim off any of the excess fabric yet.

10 If you prefer to have a plain edge with piping or cord, omit the beads and hem stitching and make up as for a cushion (see page 104–105), adding knots or tassels as wished.

11 Carefully wash and press the embroidery (see page 17).

12 To make up the pincushion, cut out the lining and backing fabric with 12 mm (½ in) seam allowances.

13 Place the lining on the back of the embroidery and cut to the same measurements as the twisted lattice band square. With as invisible stitches as possible, stitch this piece to the back of the embroidery.

14 Trim the excess hem from the open-sided square stitched edge to 12 mm (½ in). Turn in a generous 12 mm (½ in) seam allowance on the backing fabric and, with wrong sides together and the seam edge just touching the open-sided square stitches, ladder stitch the two pieces together leaving a generous opening to push in the filling pad.

15 To make a sawdust filling pad, make a small cushion (see page 104–105) of two pieces of strong calico the same measurements as the finished size of your pincushion. Three-quarters fill the calico bag with sawdust and then carefully ease into the pincushion.

16 Settle the sawdust and then completely fill the calico bag. Sew up the opening securely.

17 Ladder stitch the pincushion opening (see page 35).

KEY

	Stitch/Thread
	Kloster blocks DMC Coton Perlé No. 8, Colour 816
	Satin stitch corner and Central motif DMC Coton Perlé No. 8, Colour 816
	Twisted lattice band DMC Coton Perlé No. 8, Colour 816
	Reversed diagonal faggoting DMC Stranded Cotton, Colour 816 (2 strands)
	Square eyelets DMC Stranded Cotton, Colour 816 (2 strands)
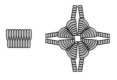	Needleweaving and Greek cross DMC Stranded Cotton, Colour 816 (2 strands)
	Open-sided square edging DMC Stranded Cotton, Colour 816 (2 strands)

SCISSORS KEEPER

This eye-catching scissors keeper will ensure your scissors are never lost. Worked in vibrant colours, or silver and gold thread, incorporating beads for pizzazz, this small item is a novelty. Add exuberant finishing touches in the manner so delightfully found in ethnic embroidery. Choose contrasting thread or exotic bead tassels, shimmering bead combinations or form knots on the cord hanging.

Finished size: 4 x 4 cm (1½ x 1½ in)

Materials

- 20.5 cm (8 in) square Minster linen, 28 threads to the inch, or evenweave of your own colour choice
- 12.5 cm (5 in) lining fabric for the embroidery
- 1 ball of DMC Coton Perlé No. 8 white or equivalent
- 1 ball of DMC Coton Perlé No. 12 white or equivalent
- 1 reel DMC Fil Argent Clair or Kreinik very fine braid 001 (optional)
- 30 cm (12 in) twisted cord
- Beading needle or Crewel No. 10
- Small pearls or seed beads to match or contrast

Method

1 Refer to the techniques section on pages 17–37. Prepare your fabric as described. (The generous allowance makes the design easier to handle.)

2 This is one occasion when the buttonhole edging may be worked first to establish the design outline. Following the chart, start your buttonhole edging, using Coton Perlé No. 8, at A, 5.5 cm (2¼ in) from the bottom and side edge. Work round the small motif before infilling the shape with kloster blocks.

3 The square eyelets are worked with Coton Perlé No. 12.

4 Cut and withdraw the threads, then needleweave with a dove's eye filling, using Coton Perlé No. 12, starting at B and following the directional arrows. In order to include the bead in the centre of the filling change the needle to fit through the bead.

5 Bring the needle and thread into the centre of the square. Thread on a bead before taking the needle down into the first bar to make the first loop. Complete this loop and the one on the second bar. Take the needle and thread back through the bead on the way to completing the third loop, so that the bead is suspended and stabilized in the centre of the square. Adjust the thread to centralize and complete the dove's eye. Repeat this as shown on the chart.

6 Carefully wash and press the embroidery (see page 17) before cutting the design away from the background. Refer to the section on cutting away from the buttonhole stitches (see page 27) before you start.

7 Make a cord of approximately 30 cm (12 in) long (see page 36) with the same threads that you have been using. Loop the cord over your scissors and bind the two ends together.

8 To make up the scissors keeper, follow the instructions for making up the heart pomander on page 58, omitting the pomander filling and oil and substituting a stuffing of lightweight wadding. Secure and stitch the bound ends of the cord to one side of the scissors keeper at the point shown on the photograph before sewing both sides together.

9 Add your chosen finishing touches, beads or an exotic tassel (see page 35–36).

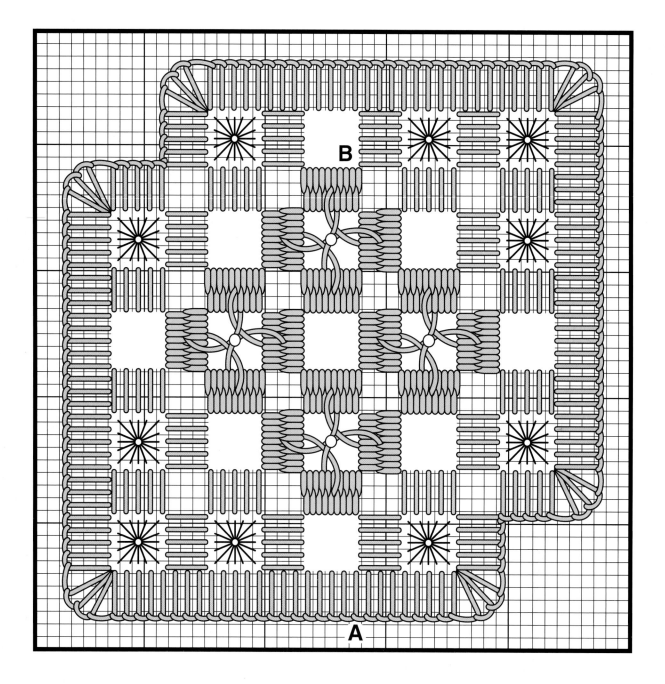

KEY

Stitch/Thread

	Kloster blocks DMC Coton Perlé No. 8 or equivalent		Square eyelets DMC Coton Perlé No. 12 or equivalent
	Buttonhole edging DMC Coton Perlé No. 8 or equivalent		Needleweaving with dove's eye filling and central bead DMC Coton Perlé No. 12 or equivalent

PHOTOGRAPH FRAME

Enjoy the harmonious design of this fresh white photograph frame in your bedroom. The design of interlocked hearts is shadowed with small satin stitch hearts and fillings of simple needleweaving and looped picots. A twisted lattice band creates an interesting textured outline to sit on the edges of the frame and border the design. A fine satin ribbon could be threaded through the twisted lattice band to create another dimension to the embroidery.

Finished size: 20 cm (7¾ in) square
Inner measurement: 10 cm (4 in) square

Materials

- 33 cm (13 in) square Minster linen, 28 threads to the inch, colour white
- 1 ball of DMC Coton Perlé No. 8 white
- 1 ball of DMC Coton Perlé No. 12 white
- Small packet of beads to match backing fabric (optional)
- Beading needle and thread (optional)
- 45 cm (18 in) square of mounting board
- 30 cm (12 in) square of fabric for backing the frame
- 30 cm (12 in) square of coloured mounting board (or fabric) for backing the embroidery
- 12.5 cm (5 in) sheet transparent plastic or acetate (optional)
- 1 m (1¼ yd) matching cord (optional)
- Picture ring for hanging or buttonhole curtain ring
- Fabric glue
- Craft knife

Method

1 Refer to the techniques section on pages 17–37. Prepare your fabric as described and tack in central horizontal and vertical lines. It would also be advisable to tack in the diagonal lines.

2 Using the Coton Perlé No. 8, start your first kloster block at A, 9 cm (3½ in) or 102 threads down from the centre point and two threads to the right of the vertical centre line. Measuring alone is not always exact so count from the centre point in twelves and mark each group of 12 with a pin or small tailor tack.

3 Following the chart, work clockwise and complete all the kloster block heart motifs.

4 Stitch the top and bottom outlining rows of twisted lattice band, followed by the small satin stitch hearts. Beads may be sewn in between the crosses of the twisted lattice band (see Sampler on page 46) if wished.

5 Work the reversed diagonal faggoting and corner eyelets with the Coton Perlé No. 12.

6 Cut and withdraw the threads inside each motif. Work simple needleweaving in the central motif, but include picots on the corner motifs, starting at B. Square filets, picot knots, dove's eye or loop filling, or spider's web could all the worked in the motifs as an alternative if preferred.

7 Carefully wash and press the embroidery (see page 17).

8 To make up the photograph mount, cut two pieces of cardboard to fit the size of the embroidery (see Fig. 1). Cut a 'window' in one piece of card to fit the centre space of the embroidery. With the embroidery face down on a clean surface, position the window mount on the back so that the coloured side shows through the embroidery.

Fig. 1 Photograph mount

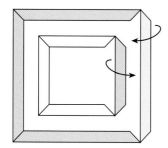

9 Fold the fabric over the edges and insert pins into the edge of the card to secure. Fold over and mitre the corners (see Fig. 1), cutting out the bulk. Apply fabric adhesive to the card and stick the fabric down. Trim the fabric to 2.5 cm (1 in).

10 Cut out the centre square of the mounted fabric leaving a 12 mm (½ in) allowance for turnings. Snip carefully, diagonally into each corner. Apply adhesive to the back outline edge of the window mount and carefully fold the fabric over to stick on the back of the card. Take care to make the right-angled corners as neat as possible on the front. The edging of twisted lattice band should be sitting on the edge of the card mount.

11 Cover the second piece of card as described, but do not cut out a window mount. Mark the positioning of the hanging ring, if using, and make a small slit through the back of the fabric and card in the centre about 5 cm (2 in) from the top edge. Push through the split pin hanging ring. Open the pins to secure it in place. If your hanging ring is one which sticks into position, stick it on once the frame is completed.

12 Cut the transparent sheet 12 mm (½ in) larger than the 'window' and place behind the window space followed by the picture and fabric-backed card (right side out). Ladder stitch (see page 35) the back and front pieces together. If you decide to glue the two sides together, use pegs to hold them in position while the glue is drying.

13 A fine cord will hide the seam if necessary, but the join will need to be overlapped and tucked in between the two pieces of card before the glue has set or the stitching completed.

KEY

Stitch/Thread

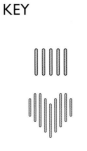

Kloster blocks
DMC Coton Perlé No. 8

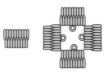

Satin stitch hearts
DMC Coton Perlé No. 8

Twisted lattice band
DMC Coton Perlé No. 8

Square eyelets
DMC Coton Perlé No. 12

Reversed diagonal faggoting
DMC Coton Perlé No. 12

Needleweaving with looped picots
DMC Coton Perlé No. 12

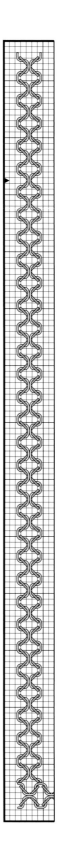

CHAPTER 3

CASES AND COVERS

The projects in this section are thoroughly practical and useful, but because they are worked in Hardanger embroidery they become exceptionally decorative whether they are in crisp white or colours. Colourways are very personal and may be changed to suit your own surroundings or themed to make a matching set.

- Spectacles cases in dark colours are utilitarian – and fun too.

- An innocent-looking pure white hanger cover disguises a hidden pocket for small valuables.

- For the bathroom or that special pine shelf, there is a delicate and fresh white edging worked with a repeating pattern to fit all lengths.

- A needlecase in cobalt blue, with matching shaded threads and a shimmering beaded edging, will encourage you to store your needles safely.

- A scissors case, complete with an elegant tassel, will protect your scissors and adorn any side table as an ornament.

- In white for the bedroom or in a soft furnishing colour, an allover pattern is worked as a cushion centrepiece that will long be admired.

SPECTACLES CASE

Glasses to protect your eyes or as a necessity will always need a case and in strong practical colours these two contemporary spectacles cases will be fun to make and use. The design is symbolically shaped with simple needleweaving giving scope to enjoy the shaded threads. Leave out the central part of the design and fill in with 'eyes' based on satin stitch stars for the minimalist look and a case with a difference.

Finished size of spectacles case: 18 x 9 cm (7 x 3½ in)
Finished size of design: 15 x 5 cm (6 x 2 in)

Materials

Blue Version
- 2 pieces of 25 x 15 cm (10 x 6 in) Jobelan evenweave, 28 threads to the inch, colour denim blue
- 1 ball of DMC Coton Perlé No. 8 colour No. 797
- 43 x 25 cm (17 x 10 in) lining fabric (e.g. silk, soft cotton, Viyella or lawn) to match

- 2 pieces of 25 x 15 cm (10 x 6 in) backing fabric to show up design
- 40.5 x 23 cm (16 x 9 in) stiff buckram
- 40.5 x 23 cm (16 x 9 in) pelmet Vilene No. 239
- 40.5 x 23 cm (16 x 9 in) Bondaweb
- 90 cm (1 yd) co-ordinating twisted cord for piping
- Caron Collection Wildflowers colour teak

Maroon Version (Fabric and Threads)
- 2 pieces of 25 x 15 cm (10 x 6 in) Zweigart Brittney linen, 28 threads to the inch, colour No. 906
- 1 ball of DMC Coton Perlé No. 8 colour No. 816
- Caron Collection Wildflowers colour passion

Method

1 Refer to the techniques section on pages 17–37. Prepare your linen as described and tack in centre lines.

2 Following the chart and using Coton Perlé No. 8, work your outline of kloster blocks starting from the centre at A.

3 Fill in the kloster blocks forming the remaining shapes and the small star. If the 'eyes' are going to be used instead, centre a square eyelet in the middle of the inner shape as shown in the picture and border with two 'arms' of the satin stitch star (see page 20).

4 With Caron Wildflowers thread, complete all the eyelets.

5 Cut and withdraw the threads to start needleweaving the top shape at B and the side small diamond shapes

at C. Although a dove's eye is shown in the chart in this shape, picot knots, looped picots or a spider's web would also be suitable.

6 Turn the work to complete the other end in the same way.

7 Carefully wash and press the embroidery (see page 17).

8 Cut the two pieces of buckram and Vilene to the same size as the template.

9 Mark the outline of the template on the backing paper of the Bondaweb. Cut out and iron on to the wrong side of the backing fabric (following the manufacturer's instructions). Peel off the paper, cover the right side of the backing with baking parchment for protection and bond to one piece of buckram. Cover both pieces of buckram in this way.

10 With the embroidery face down, place the fabric-covered buckram behind the embroidery, followed by the Vilene. Look to the front, centre the design over the stiffening and check the fabric is straight.

11 Leaving a 1.5 cm (⅝ in) seam allowance, trim off the excess material. Turn the allowance over the Vilene, making small shaped pleats round the angled corners, adjust the fabric and pull firmly. Tack and sew down with herringbone stitch (see Fig. 1). Repeat for the other side of the case.

12 Cut the lining fabric 12 mm (½ in) larger than the template and place it on top of the Vilene.

13 Turn under the seam allowance, tack and slip stitch into position about 2 mm (¹⁄₁₆ in) in from the edge, adjusting the lining so that there are no wrinkles.

14 At the opening end, adjust the lining to sit on the lip edge so that the seam will be hidden once the cord is sewn on. Repeat the process on the other side.

15 To make up the case, ladder stitch the two 'sandwiches' together (with lining sides facing each other), starting in the middle at the bottom of the case. Work up each side in turn stopping about 2.5 cm (1 in) away from the lip so that you can neatly hide and sew the ends of the cord in the seam.

16 Sew one end of the cord into the side seam and, following the directional arrows in Fig. 2, pin the cord (see page 36) to border the case. Finish off by tucking the end of the cord into the side seam and sewing firmly into position.

17 Complete the ladder stitching up the side seams with extra stitches near the opening for strength before stitching the cord into position.

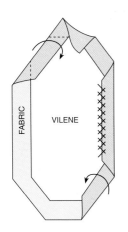

Fig. 1 Herringbone on wrong side

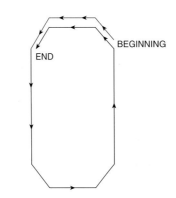

Fig. 2 Direction of a cord

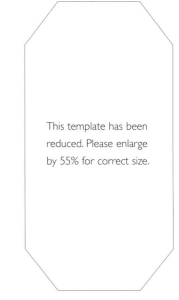

This template has been reduced. Please enlarge by 55% for correct size.

Fig. 3 Specatacles case template

KEY

Stitch/Thread

Kloster blocks
DMC Coton Perlé No. 8,
Colour No. 797

Simple star or 'eyes'
DMC Coton Perlé No. 8,
Colour No. 797
(Maroon Version, Colour
Passion)

Square eyelets
Caron Collection
Wildflowers Colour
Teak (Maroon Version,
Colour Passion)

Needleweaving and dove's
eye filling
Caron Collection
Wildflowers Colour
Teak (Maroon Version,
Colour Passion)

HANGER COVER

This is a hanger cover with a difference. It actually provides a safe haven for your jewellery and small valuables. Stitching together at the bottom with just a central opening forms a secret container pocket in which to hide small items. The border design of simple needleweaving has a central motif which is visible when the clothes are hung up. If you wished, a matching pomander could be worked by stitching the small central motif with twisted bars and outlining it with buttonhole edging instead of kloster blocks. Follow the instructions for making up the heart pomander on page 58.

Finished size: 42 x 10 cm (16½ x 4 in)

Materials

White Version
- 2 pieces of 53.5 x 20.5 cm (21 x 8 in) Zweigart Lugana, 25 threads to the inch, white
- 1 ball of DMC Coton Perlé No. 8 white
- 1 ball of DMC Coton Perlé No. 12 white
- Padded wooden hanger (about 43 cm/17 in)

- 53.5 x 20.5 cm (21 x 8 in) lightweight lining fabric to match or contrast
- 12.5 cm (5 in) Velcro

Cream Version (Fabric and Threads)
- 2 pieces of 53.5 x 20.5 cm (21 x 8 in) Zweigart Lugana, 25 threads to the inch, colour No.252
- 1 ball of Anchor pearl cotton No. 8 colour No. 386
- 1 skein Anchor stranded cotton colour No. 386

Method

1 Refer to the techniques section on pages 17–37. Prepare your fabric as described. Tack in the central vertical line on both pieces of fabric.

2 Taking one side of fabric, start stitching your kloster block border at A, 5 cm (2 in) from the bottom and 5.2 cm (2⅛ in) from the right-hand edge using Coton Perlé No. 8. Following the chart, work to the centre and repeat for the other half of the hanger so that you have 27 kloster blocks sitting along the bottom line.

3 Complete the central motif shape and, taking Coton Perlé No. 12 or two strands of the stranded cotton, stitch the reversed diagonal faggoting.

4 Cut and withdraw the threads from the border a few inches at a time and needleweave with Coton Perlé No. 12 or two strands of the stranded cotton starting at B.

5 Cut and withdraw the threads from the central shape and, referring to the chart, start at C to needleweave with twisted bars (and picot knots if wished) in the top motif following the directional arrows. Simple needleweaving is worked in the other shapes starting at D. Other fillings may be substituted if preferred. One or both sides may be embroidered.

6 To make the hem, count eight threads from the kloster blocks and work a back stitch (use Coton Perlé No. 8) with one row of open-sided square edging stitch (see page 32) to the measurements on the template (see step 8). Trim the fabric leaving 6 mm (¼ in) seam allowance.

7 Carefully wash and press the embroidery (see page 17).

8 As wooden hangers come in different lengths and curves, make a template from your own hanger. Place the hanger on a piece of old cotton fabric and draw the outline curved shape on the fabric, adding on 12 mm (½ in) allowance at each end for 'take-up'. Cut out the template with the depth of the hanger from the hook to the hem measuring 10 cm (4 in) and completely straight along the bottom edge.

9 Cut the lining, back piece and embroidered piece to the same size as the template adding 12 mm (½ in) seam allowance round the hanger curve and sides only.

10 Place the lining behind the embroidered piece of fabric and tack together. Take the back piece and, with right sides facing, tack and machine the outline of the hanger. Stitch through all three thicknesses, leaving the bottom open and a small gap in the centre top for the metal hook. Trim the seam, oversew, turn the right way round and press.

11 Turn up the hem of the lining, level with the inner edge of the open-sided square edging stitch, and slip stitch the two pieces together.

12 Stitch the Velcro, centrally, to either side of the inside of the hanger.

13 Turn up the hem of the back piece of the cover level with the inner edge of the open-sided square edging stitch. Trim the excess and tack together, either side of the Velcro.

14 Pin stitch or hem stitch (see page 31 and 32) the two edges together using the clusters already formed.

KEY

Stitch/Thread

Kloster blocks and satin stitch motif
Anchor Pearl Cotton No. 8 Colour 386
(DMC Coton Perlé No. 8 white)

Reversed diagonal faggoting
2 strands Anchor Stranded Cotton,
Colour No. 386 (DMC Coton Perlé
No. 12 white)

Needleweaving with twisted bars
2 strands Anchor Stranded Cotton,
Colour No. 386 (DMC Coton Perlé
No. 12 white)

Back stitch picot with open square sided stitch
Anchor Pearl Cotton No. 8, Colour 386
2 strands anchor Stranded Cotton, Colour
No. 386 (DMC Coton Perlé No. 12 white)

SHELF EDGING

Practical and attractive, this simple shelf edging cover will trim anything from your kitchen pine dresser to your bathroom cupboard. Take the idea a little further and make it a border for a bridge cloth or tablecloth where you want the cloth to fit exactly on the edges rather than hang freely. Greek cross fillings show up strongly in the repeating design, but diagonal twisted bars could be substituted.

Finished size: work to suit your own requirements Pattern repeat for 28 threads to the inch: 80 threads or 7.2 cm (2⅞ in) plus length of beginning and end of design 46 threads or 4.2 cm (1⅝ in)

Materials

- Length: number of repeats for shelf measurement plus beginning and end of design plus 5 cm (2 in) extra each end for handling
- Width: width of shelf plus 12 mm (½ in) hem allowance plus drop of 60 threads or 5.2 cm (2⅛ in) plus 5 cm (2 in) extra each side for handling
- Minster linen, 28 threads to the inch, colour white
- 1 ball of DMC Coton Perlé No. 8 white
- 1 ball of DMC Coton Perlé No. 12 white

Method

1 Refer to the techniques section on pages 17–37. Prepare your fabric as described and tack in the vertical centre line.

2 Using the Coton Perlé No. 8, start your first straight line kloster block at a point A, leaving 5 cm (2 in) handling fabric on the right-hand side edge and your allowance for the width of the shelf. Turn the book so that as you look at the chart the edge points are facing upwards.

3 As you stitch the straight line, fill in the inner and outer diamond points. This will help you not to miscount. Echo the first straight line with a second one.

4 Stitch the square motif between each diamond following the chart.

5 Turn the work and complete the outline buttonhole edging. There are no square eyelets in this design in the buttonhole edging but, if you prefer, eyelets may be added at this stage.

6 Turn the work back again with the points facing upwards to complete all the reversed diagonal faggoting and needleweaving using Coton Perlé No. 12.

7 Cut and withdraw the threads in the small half-diamond shapes, one shape at a time, and needleweave the bars with Coton Perlé No. 12. starting at B.

8 Cut and withdraw the threads in the small square motif. Needleweave the bars and include a Greek cross filling as shown starting at C, or woven and twisted bars (see page 29) if you prefer.

9 Continue from the end of the buttonhole edging and stitch a small hem round the remaining three sides of the shelf edging to the required width of your shelf.

10 Carefully wash and press the embroidery (see page 17) before cutting the design away from the background. Refer to the section on cutting away from the buttonhole stitches (see page 27) before you start.

KEY

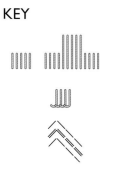

Stitch/Thread

Kloster blocks and satin stitch motif
DMC Coton Perlé No. 8

Buttonhole edging
DMC Coton Perlé No. 8

Reversed diagonal faggoting
DMC Coton Perlé No. 12

Needleweaving
DMC Coton Perlé No. 12

Greek cross filling
DMC Coton Perlé No. 12

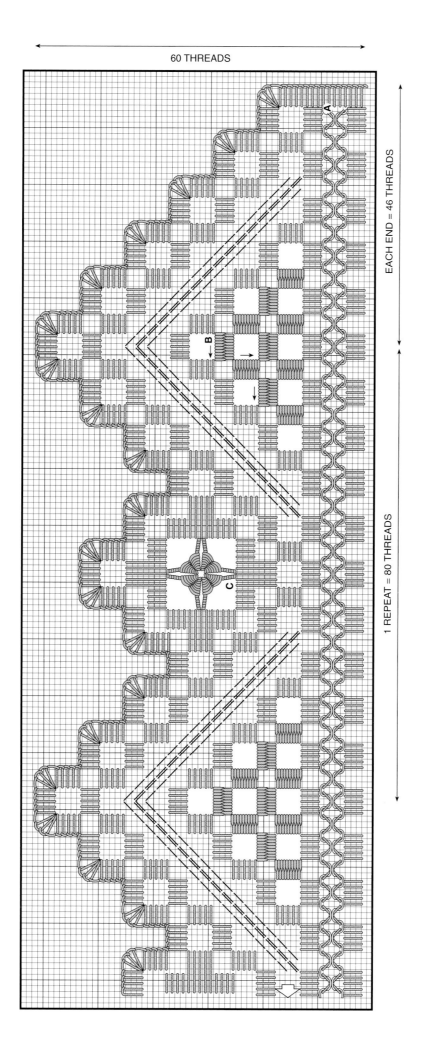

60 THREADS

EACH END = 46 THREADS

1 REPEAT = 80 THREADS

A

B

C

93

NEEDLECASE

A simple rectangle folded into three makes up this practical and pretty envelope-style needlecase. Soft blues are embellished with beads which add a little sparkle and make it hard to lose. Simple needleweaving on the top of the flap contrasts with the more decorative half Greek cross filling and the traditional satin stitch star with eyelets gives a strong focal point. Hem edging with beads is a quick and interesting finish to the needlecase.

Finished size (open): 21 x 10.5 cm (8¼ x 4¼ in)

Materials

- 26.5 x 19 cm (10½ x 7½ in) Jobelan evenweave, 28 threads to the inch, colour No. 41 Nordic blue
- 1 ball of DMC Coton Perlé No. 8 colour No. 798
- Caron Collection Wildflower colour blue lavender
- 75 blue seed beads
- Beading needle and thread to match project
- 12 x 10 cm (5 x 4 in) soft white cotton fabric for inside the case

Method

1 Refer to the techniques section on pages 17–37. Prepare your linen as described and tack in the central vertical line.

2 Following the chart and using Coton Perlé No. 8, start the kloster blocks with your first stitch at A, 4.5 cm (1¾ in) up from the bottom edge, and two threads to the right of the vertical central line, and establish the 'V' shape of the design.

3 Echo the inner 'V' shape and the rest of the design with kloster blocks and work the satin stitch star motif.

4 Stitch the buttonhole outline, remembering to take the stitches straight along the edge to the fold of the flap.

5 Stitch all the eyelets and reversed diagonal faggoting with the Caron Collection Wildflower thread.

6 Cut and withdraw the threads for the needleweaving.

7 Following the chart, work the Greek cross filling starting at B.

8 Turn the work upside-down to start your needleweaving at C (upside-down on the chart).

9 To make the beaded edge, follow the method described on page 33, but in this instance do not pull

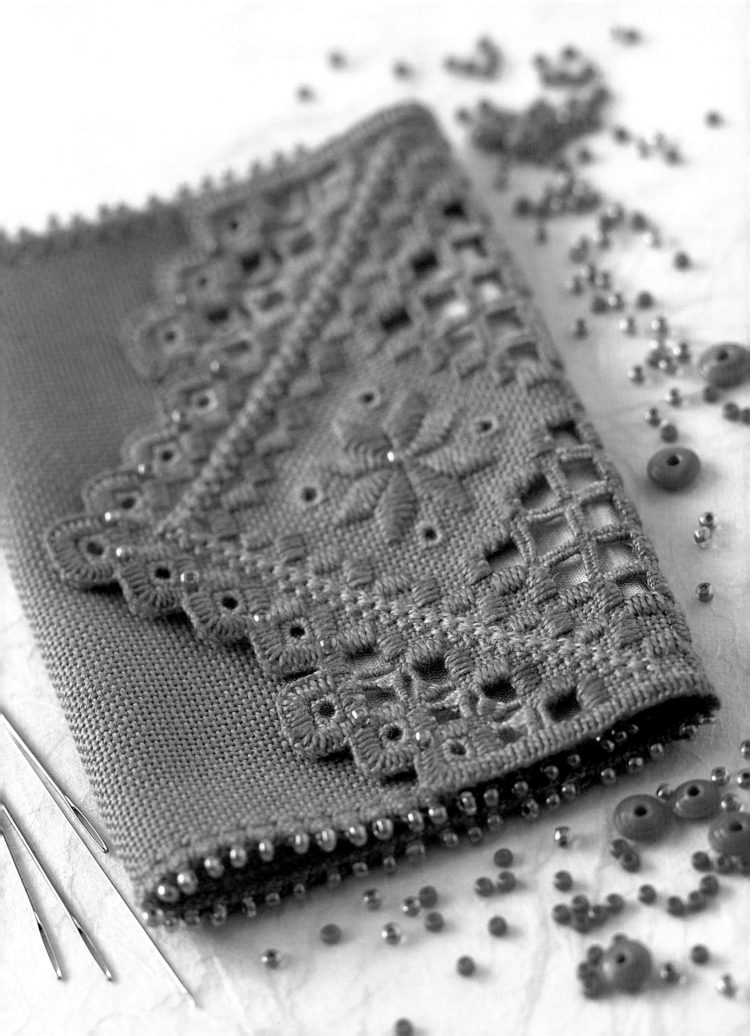

a fabric thread. Start your first back stitch next to the last buttonhole stitch (in the next four threads and working in the same line). Stitch for 14 cm (5½ in) before turning to work the short straight edge. Remember to mitre the corners (see page 30). Do not put beads on the short straight end, but work normal back stitch with open-sided square edging stitch using the Coton Perlé No. 8 colour 798.

10 Finger press the fold so that the beads are sitting upright on the edge. Secure the hem with one row of open-sided square edging stitch using Coton Perlé No. 8 Colour 798 (to match the buttonhole edging when the needlecase is folded). Trim off the excess fabric close to the hem.

11 Carefully wash and press the embroidery (see page 17) before cutting the envelope flap away from the background. Refer to the section on cutting away from the buttonhole stitches (see page 27) before you start.

12 Pink or machine zigzag the edges of the light wool or flannel for your needles before sewing into position with a back stitch along the first fold line about 6 cm (2½ in) from the straight edge.

13 Additional beads may be sewn on the corner point of each buttonhole step.

14 Fasten the needlecase with wrap-around ribbon ties or a small loop and button or bead.

KEY

	Stitch/Thread
	Kloster blocks DMC Coton Perlé No. 8, Colour 798
	Satin stitch star DMC Coton Perlé No. 8, Colour 798
	Buttonhole edging DMC Coton Perlé No. 8, Colour 798
	Reversed diagonal faggoting Caron Collection Watercolours, Colour Blue Lavender
	Square eyelets Caron Collection Watercolours, Colour Blue Lavender
	Needleweaving and Greek cross filling Caron Collection Watercolours, Colour Blue Lavender
	Open sided square edging DMC Coton Perlé No. 8, Colour 798

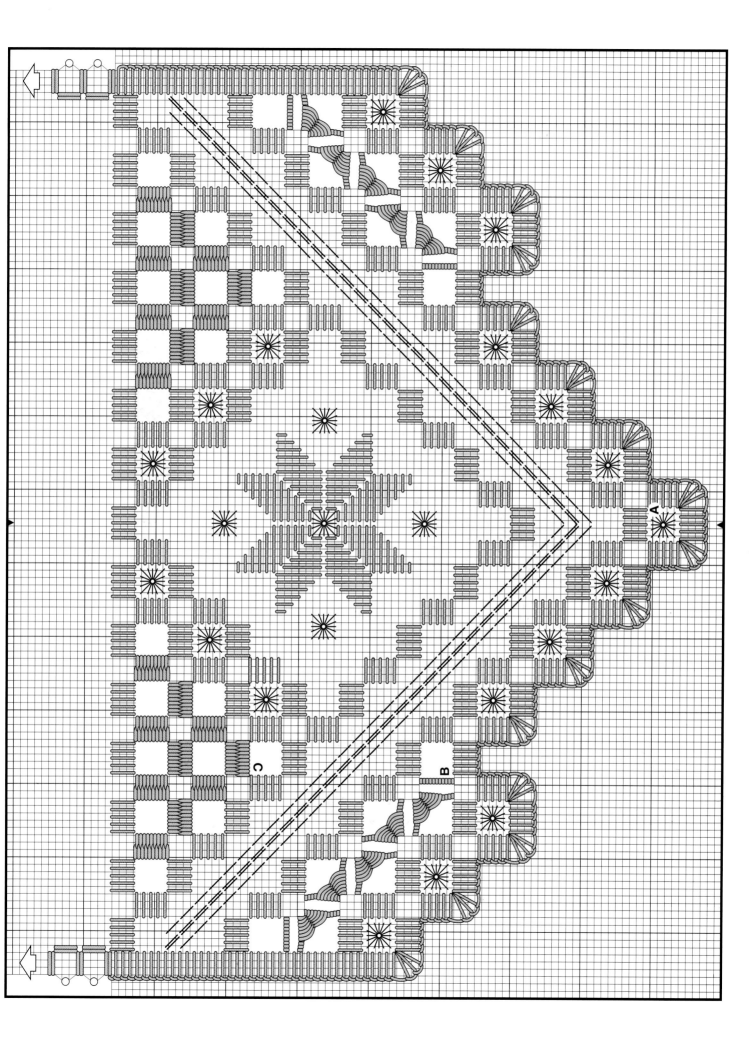

SCISSORS CASE

With beads adding a touch of luxury, keep those precious, favourite scissors in this beautiful case and display it as an ornament. Add a twisted cord and exotic tassel and it will hang from the wall as a decoration. Basic kloster blocks and buttonhole edging outline the area to be cut and embroidered. The square filet filling lightens the design.

Finished size: 7 x 10 cm (2¾ x 4 in)

Materials

- 30 x 20.5 cm (12 x 8 in) Minster linen, 28 threads to the inch, colour white
- 20.5 x 18 cm (8 x 7 in) backing fabric for the embroidery
- 20.5 x 18 cm (8 x 7 in) lining fabric
- 20.5 x 18 cm (8 x 7 in) pelmet Vilene No. 239
- 20.5 x 18 cm (8 x 7 in) Bondaweb or fusible web
- 1 ball of DMC Coton Perlé No. 8 white
- 1 ball of DMC Coton Perlé No. 12 white

Method

1 Refer to the techniques section on pages 17–37. Prepare your fabric as described. (The generous fabric allowance makes the small design easier to handle and sew.)

2 With the short length facing you at the bottom, start your first kloster block at A, 5.5 cm (2¼ in) up from the bottom edge and 10 cm (4 in) from the right-hand side edge.

3 Using the Coton Perlé No. 8 and following the chart, stitch the diagonal line of kloster blocks. Then turn to work the second side of blocks, followed by the third side. At this stage leave out the blocks which 'link' the outline to the buttonhole edging, because it will be easier to fill these in later.

4 Outline the whole shape with the buttonhole edging and then fill in the single 'linking' blocks. Now that there are kloster blocks either side you will be able to run through both outlines to reach the subsequent block without any unsightly long threads on the back.

5 Using Coton Perlé No. 12, work the square eyelets.

6 Cut and withdraw the threads, a small area at a time to keep it stable.

7 With Coton Perlé No. 12, start needleweaving the bars at B following the directional arrows.

8 Continue with the needleweaving and include the square filet filling (see page 27) as shown on the chart. Picot knots, looped picots, dove's eyes with or without beads (see page 70), square filets or spider's webs could be substituted.

9 Starting 12 mm (½ in) above the front, complete the back as for the front working the outline, buttonhole edging and square eyelets, adding the fastening, but omitting the needleweaving.

10 Carefully wash and press the embroidery (see page 17) before cutting the design away from the background. Refer to the section on cutting away from the buttonhole stitches (see page 27) before you start. Cut the two pieces of

11 Vilene to the same size as the template.

12 Mark the outline of the template on the backing paper of the Bondaweb or fusible web. Cut out and iron (following the manufacturer's instructions) onto the wrong side of the backing fabric. Peel off the paper, cover the right side of the backing with baking parchment for protection and bond to one piece of Vilene. Cover both pieces in this way.

13 Cut two pieces of lining fabric to the same size as the template (Fig.1), but adding 12 mm (½ in) to the straight top edge. As before, iron Bondaweb or fusible web on to the back of the lining. Make a 'sandwich' and bond the lining piece to the uncovered side of the

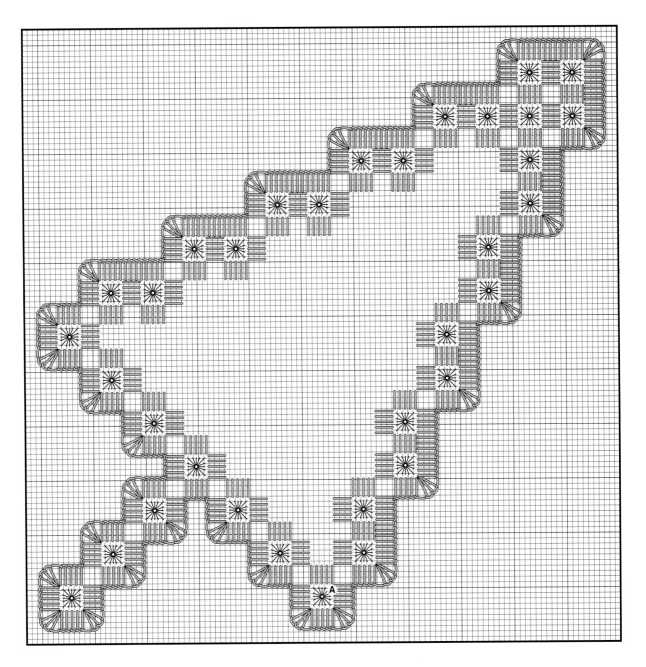

Vilene (already bonded with the backing fabric) turning the 12 mm (½ in) allowance over to cover the top straight raw edge. Iron to bond into place. It is important to cover this top edge as a raw edge would be noticed.

14 With the embroidery face down, place the backing-covered Vilene piece behind the embroidery. Centre the design over the stiffening and check the fabric is straight. Slip stitch the two together, trimming off any excess which is showing from the front. Repeat for the back.

15 To make up the case, place the two sides together (lining sides facing each other) and back stitch together up the side seams. To place less strain on the buttonhole edging, back stitch round the inside of the buttonhole edging and also oversew the outside edges of the buttonhole edging together.

16 Complete the back stitching, with extra stitches near the opening for strength.

17 Add the finishing touches as you prefer – a button and loop, bead, tassel or press stud for the fastening, a twisted cord (see page 36) for hanging or an exotic tassel (see page 35) for fun.

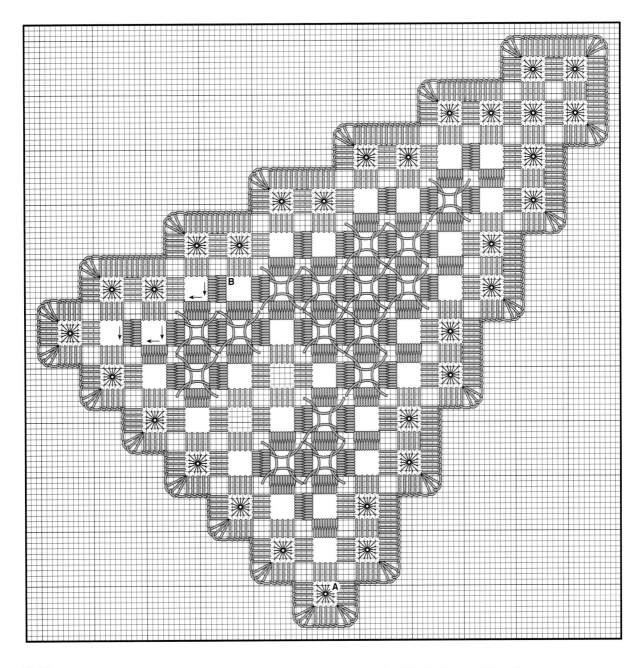

KEY

Stitch/Thread

 Kloster blocks
DMC Coton Perlé No. 8 white

 Buttonhole edging
DMC Coton Perlé No. 8 white

 Square eyelets
DMC Coton Perlé No. 12 white

 Needleweaving with square filets
DMC Coton Perlé No. 12 white

This template has been reduced. Please enlarge by 50% for correct size.

Fig. 1 Template for scissor case lining

CUSHION COVER

Cushions add character and interesting detail to any interior. Fresh white or in cool colours to match your furnishings and decor, this all-over repeating design is inspired by the patterns found on the beautiful mosaic floor in St Mark's Basilica, Venice. Diagonal lines of kloster blocks link a basic Hardanger shape to form a secondary pattern containing the traditional Hardanger star motif, with simple picot knots adding texture to the needleweaving. This is a simple square cushion with piping or edged with cord.

Finished size of cushion: 33 cm (13 in) square
Finished size of white cushion design: 22.5 cm (8¾ in)
Finished size of twilight blue cushion design: 20.5 cm (8 in)

Materials

White Version
- 45 cm (18 in) square Zweigart Lugana, 25 threads to the inch, colour No. 100 white
- 1 ball of DMC Coton Perlé No. 8 white
- 1 ball of DMC Coton Perlé No. 12 white
- 45 cm (18 in) cotton contrasting fabric to line embroidery
- 70 cm (27½ in) backing fabric and thread to match for cushion
- 2 m (2½ yd) medium thickness white cord
- 35.5 cm (14 in) cushion pad

Twilight Blue Version (Fabric and Threads)
- 45 cm (18 in) square Minster linen, 28 threads to the inch, colour No. 411 twilight blue
- 45 cm (18 in) cotton contrasting fabric to line embroidery
- 70 cm (27½ in) backing fabric and thread to match for cushion
- 1 ball of DMC Coton Perlé No. 8 white
- 1 ball of DMC Coton Perlé No. 12 white
- 1 ball of DMC Coton Perlé No. 8 colour No. 927
- 1 ball of DMC Coton Perlé No. 12 colour No. 927

Method

1 If you are working the twilight blue, or substituting a colour of your own choice, use the chart to check where the colours are used. Refer to the techniques section on pages 17–37. Prepare your linen as described and tack in centre lines in both directions.

2 Using Coton Perlé No. 8, follow the chart and start the kloster blocks with your first stitch at A, 14 threads down from the centre point and two threads to the right of the vertical centre line.

3 Work all the kloster blocks forming the small central diamond shape to establish the first part of the design. At this stage it may help you to sew in a grid of tacking lines (vertically and horizontally), 32 threads apart, in order to check that your design is correct and that you do not miscount any blocks.

4 Thereafter, following the chart, consistently 'grow' the lines of kloster blocks from this diamond shape to create the repeating all-over pattern.

5 Using the Coton Perlé No. 8, complete all the central star motifs and both twisted lattice bands.

6 Using Coton Perlé No. 12, stitch all the eyelets in the kloster block squares, in the centre of each star and around each star motif. As you will see from the photograph, there are two small variations on the

twilight blue and white version. The eyelets round the star motifs are positioned differently (see the position of eyelets on the chart for the needlecase, page 97) and a pearl has been sewn in the centre instead of eyelets, giving a slightly different effect to the finished piece. If pearls are to be included, sew them on last of all.

7 Cut and withdraw the threads from the small diamond shape, referring to the chart.

8 Needleweave the bars using Coton Perlé No. 12, incorporating the picot knots (or a filling of your choice) on the bars starting at B.

9 Complete the border with a line of four-sided stitch worked between the two twisted lattice bands with the Coton Perlé No. 12.

10 Carefully wash and press the embroidery (see page 17) before making up the cushion.

11 To make a well-fitting cushion, the pad should be 2.5 cm (1 in) larger than the finished fabric square. For a 35.5 cm (14 in) pad, cut the worked piece of fabric to measure 35.5 cm (14 in) square, allowing 12 mm (½ in) for the seams.

12 Cut the backing to the same size as the front and cover the piping cord with a bias-cut strip of fabric.

13 Place the fabric-covered piping cord on the right side of the backing fabric. Machine into position with a piping or zip foot, making any join as neat as possible. To join, either cut away the excess amount of piping cord and cross one end of the cord over the other to overlap neatly, or join piping fabric to fit the side measurements, butt the ends of the cord together where they meet and cut off the excess. Machine in place.

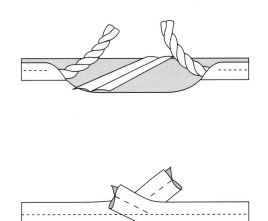

Fig. 1 Piping cut on bias

14 Place the right sides together and machine round all sides, leaving an opening (on the bottom) large enough to take the pad. Oversew and neaten the seams.

15 Turn inside out, push out the corners properly and fill with the pad.

16 Use ladder stitch to sew up the opening. If you would prefer a zip opening, insert the zip across the centre of the backing fabric, before joining to the front. Zips on a side edge can spoil the look of the cushion if they are not done neatly.

17 Refer to page 36 to attach a cord. As you reach the corner make a small overhand knot, leaving a loop, before continuing down the next side. Whip each end of the cord to prevent fraying and at the last corner lose the ends in the overhand knot at the back. Secure with stitching.

18 If you prefer to have simple tassels on each corner, loop tassel threads over the cord at the corner and bind round the heading. Wrap the cord join and hide under a tassel head at a corner.

KEY

Stitch/Thread

Kloster blocks
DMC Coton Perlé No. 8 white

Satin stitch star
DMC Coton Perlé No. 8 white (Twilight
Blue version Colour 927)

Twisted lattice band
DMC Coton Perlé No. 8 white

Square eyelets
DMC Coton Perlé No. 12 white
(Twilight Blue version Colour 927

Neeleweaving with picot knots
DMC Coton Perlee No. 12 white

Four-sided stitch
DMC Coton Perlé No. 12 white
(Twilight Blue version Colour 927)

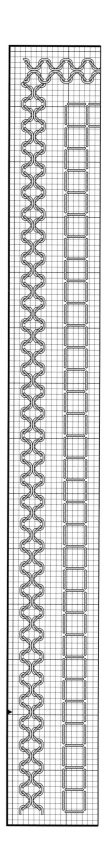

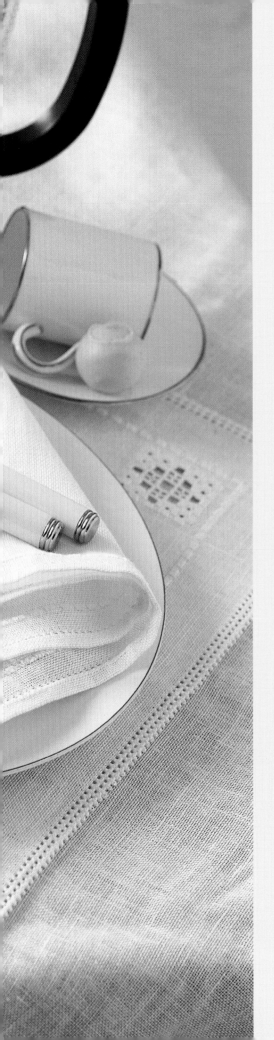

CHAPTER 4

THE PERFECT SETTING

THE CLASSIC, FRESH SIMPLICITY OF WHITE ON WHITE IS UNIVERSALLY APPRECIATED AND OFFSETS CHINA AND CUTLERY TO PERFECTION. THE HARDANGER PROJECTS IN THIS CHAPTER ECHO THIS CONCEPT. ALL THE CORNER DESIGNS IN THE TABLE SETTING PROJECTS COMPLEMENT EACH OTHER AND ARE INTERCHANGEABLE. YOU MAY PREFER TO MAKE A COMPLETE MATCHING SET WITH THE DESIGN YOU LIKE THE MOST. TOUCHES OF COLOUR CREATE A DIFFERENT IMPRESSION AND VARIATIONS.

- On soft pastel pink with white Hardanger embroidery, a small dressing-table mat will decorate any surface with simplicity and femininity.

- Present your bread rolls in a striking bread-basket cloth.

- A desirable and classic white place mat will always be in demand.

- Add elegance to the coffee tray with a cover for your cafetière worked in creams or naturals.

- Napkin rings in white, and colour variations too, will complement any of the table linen.

- Complete the look with traditional white linen table napkins or make a statement with Christmas red.

- A traditional white tablecloth is suitable for any occasion.

DRESSING-TABLE MAT

This small mat with white Hardanger embroidery, delicate square filet fillings and picot knots on a soft pink fabric will adorn any surface in your bedroom or bathroom, or could even be used to decorate your walls as a hanging. The light lacy look is further enhanced by the central motif where the 'arms' of the traditional ship motif have been adapted to touch, and form a small heart shape which encloses the diagonal eyelet. Add repeats to turn it into a tray cloth or runner.

Finished size: 20 cm (7¾ in) square

Materials

- 30 cm (12 in) square Zweigart Lugana, 25 threads to the inch, colour No. 411 pale pink
- 1 ball of DMC Coton Perlé No. 8 white
- 1 ball of DMC Coton Perlé No. 12 white

Method

1 Refer to the techniques section on pages 17–37. Prepare your linen as described and tack in centre lines in both directions. It will also be advisable to tack in the diagonal lines as shown on the chart. This will not only help you check you are correct as you work round the design but will also be a guide for lining up the central motif.

2 Using the Coton Perlé No. 8, start your first kloster block at A, 9.2 cm (3⅝ in) down from the centre point and two threads to the right of the vertical centre line.

3 Follow the design outline as shown on the chart by a broken line. You will see that there are a series of different length zigzags as the basis for the design which are not complicated.

4 Once you have returned to the beginning, go back and fill in the other shapes of kloster blocks which make up the design.

5 Outline the whole design with the buttonhole edging.

6 Still using the Coton Perlé No. 8, work the centre ship motif.

7 Using Coton Perlé No. 12, stitch all the eyelets round the design and in the centre, if you wish.

8 Using Coton Perlé No. 12, stitch the reversed diagonal faggoting, starting at a mitred point and working as shown on page 19.

9 Cut and withdraw the threads from the small diamond shapes on the centre lines (at north, south, east and west) one shape at a time. Using Coton Perlé No. 12, needleweave the bars starting at B and centre a knot or picot on the side of the bar facing towards the middle of each square.

10 Cut and withdraw threads from the corner shape and start needleweaving the bars at C. (Refer to pages 12 and 16 to remind yourself about filling larger areas with needleweaving.) This first row will just be plain needleweaving and, as usual, the bars are worked in steps as shown by the directional arrows. At the end of the line finish off your thread and start again at D. Complete the first bar then needleweave the second bar, remembering to put on a knot or picot in the middle. This second bar now completes a square of needlewoven bars and the square filet filling is worked before moving on to the third bar. Again, remember to work a knot or picot in the middle of the third bar before moving on to complete the fourth bar and another filet.

11 Row E is a diagonal row of needleweaving and a knot or picot in the middle of the second and third bars.

12 Repeat rows D and E. Continuing in this manner will ensure that the filets will all cross in exactly the same way. You will then see a beautiful secondary pattern occurring where the points meet. The last row F omits the knot or picot on the second and third bar.

13 Carefully wash and press the embroidery (see page 17) before cutting the design away from the background. Refer to the section on cutting away from the buttonhole stitches (see page 27) before you start.

KEY

	Stitch/Thread
	Kloster blocks DMC Coton Perlé No. 8
	Buttonhole edging DMC Coton Perlé No. 8
	Satin stitch ship motif DMC Coton Perlé No. 8
	Reversed diagonal faggoting DMC Coton Perlé No. 12
	Square eyelets and diagonal eyelets DMC Coton Perlé No. 12
	Needleweaving with picot knots and square filet filling DMC Coton Perlé No. 12

BREAD-BASKET CLOTH

With bold blue and white Hardanger embroidery on this simple cloth, you can present your warm bread rolls, croissants, brioches or exotic breads and conjure up recollections of long, lazy enjoyable meals spent in sunny Provence. Create your own mood by changing the colour scheme to match your pottery or china. Simple needleweaving and reversed diagonal faggoting create a striped effect in each of the corners.

Finished size: 45 cm (18 in) square
Finished design size: 42.2 cm (16⅝ in) square

Materials

Blue and White Version
- 56 cm (22 in) square Minster linen, 28 threads to the inch, colour white
- 1 ball of DMC Coton Perlé No. 8 No. 797 Blue
- 1 ball of DMC Coton Perlé No. 12 white

White Version
- 56 cm (22 in) square Zweigart Lugana, 25 threads to the inch, colour white
- 1 ball of DMC Coton Perlé No. 8 white
- 1 ball of DMC Coton Perlé No. 12 white

Method

1 Refer to the techniques section on pages 17–37. Prepare your linen as described. To change the dimensions of the mat, refer to page 16.

2 Lay the fabric flat in front of you and find the starting point A at the bottom right-hand corner – 7 cm (2¾ in) in from the lower edge of the fabric and 7.2 cm (2⅞ in) in from the right-hand side edge.

3 Start your first kloster block at A using Coton Perlé No. 8 (blue 797) and, following the chart, stitch the outline of the first corner triangle. Fill in the rest of the design with the diagonal lines of kloster blocks as shown. Let the rest of the design 'grow' from this first corner.

4 Stitch the straight line of kloster blocks to link with the subsequent corner. For the 28-count linen you will need 60 kloster blocks from corner to corner but with the 25-count Lugana you will need 52 kloster blocks from corner to corner.

5 Either complete the corner design as you get to it or just stitch the triangle outline before moving on to the following corner.

6 After completing the kloster blocks in all the corners, change your thread to Coton Perlé No. 12 white to work the reversed diagonal faggoting.

7 Only cut and withdraw the threads for needleweaving in the corner in which you are working. Begin the needleweaving at B, following the directional arrows on the chart. Complete each line of needleweaving before cutting and moving on to another (C).

8 Knots or picots could be added to the bars if you preferred, and if you want more embroidery on your corners, simply repeat the lines of pattern. Half Greek cross filling could also be substituted in the design.

9 To make up the hem, follow all the instructions for completing the hem on page 30 and mitre the corners. Tack the hem 12 threads from the outline of kloster blocks round the whole square (pin stitch hemming will be worked in this line).

10 Count eight threads for the actual hem turnings, with an inside turning of seven threads. As the fabric will fray, only cut one side at a time.

11 Use Coton Perlé No. 12 white to secure the hem with pin stitch (see page 32).

12 Wash and press the work (see page 17).

KEY

Stitch/Thread

Kloster blocks
DMC Coton Perlé No. 8 white

Reversed diagonal faggoting
DMC Coton Perlé No. 12 white

Needleweaving
DMC Coton Perlé No. 12 white

Pin stitch
DMC Coton Perlé No. 12 white

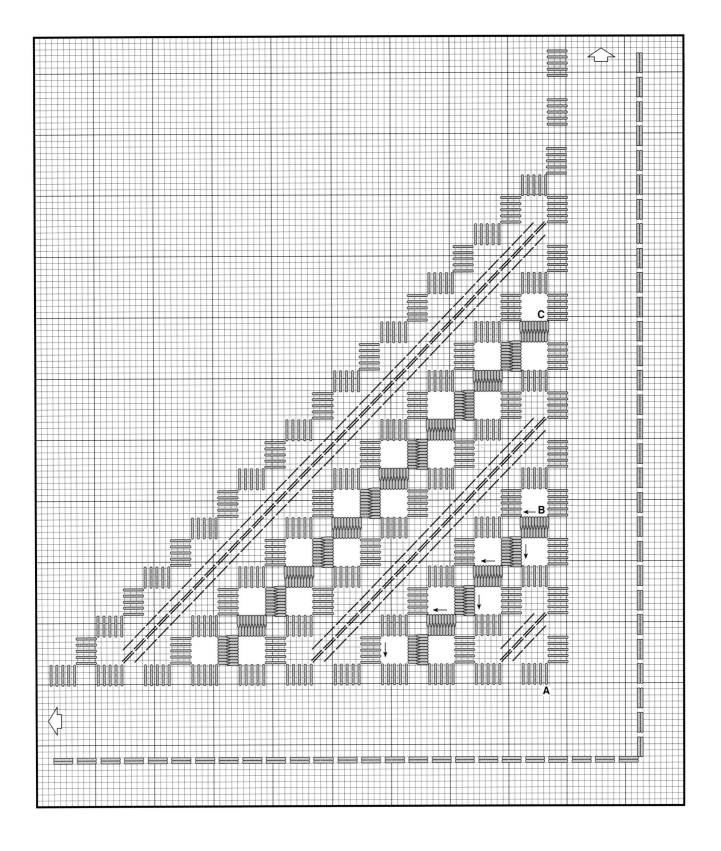

PLACE MAT

Create an impression with this superb place mat. Its classic design will grace any table, elegantly setting off your china and glass. The small, simple square motifs 'frame' your plate, with the dove's eye (or loop filling stitch) adding a lacy quality to soften the shape. The small square motif can be worked on one, two, three or four corners as necessary. Making a set of mats with different fillings on each one would not only be fun and interesting, but an excellent way of learning and practising.

Finished size: 40.5 x 29 cm (16 x 11½ in)

Materials

- 51 x 39 cm (20 x 15½ in) Minster linen, 28 threads to the inch, colour white
- 1 ball of DMC Coton Perlé No. 8 white
- 1 ball of DMC Coton Perlé No. 12 white

Method

1 Refer to the techniques section on pages 17–37. Prepare your fabric as described.

2 Lay the fabric flat in front of you and find the starting point A at the bottom right-hand corner, 9.5 cm (3¾ in) in from the lower edge of the fabric and 9.8 cm (3⅞ in) in from the right-hand side edge.

3 Start your first kloster block at A using Coton Perlé No. 8 and work the outline square shape of the first corner. Fill in the rest of the design with the kloster blocks as shown on the chart.

4 Stitch the straight line of kloster blocks forming the outline square and linking with the subsequent corner. You will need 46 kloster blocks from corner to corner on the long side and 30 kloster blocks on the short side. (If you are having difficulty with the counting, refer to the instructions on page 16).

5 After completing the kloster blocks in all the corners, change your thread to Coton Perlé No. 12 to work the squared eyelets.

6 Only cut and withdraw the threads for needleweaving in the corner in which you are working. Begin the needleweaving at B, following the directional arrows on the chart. Complete each diagonal line of needleweaving, remembering to include the dove's eye (or loop filling) as shown.

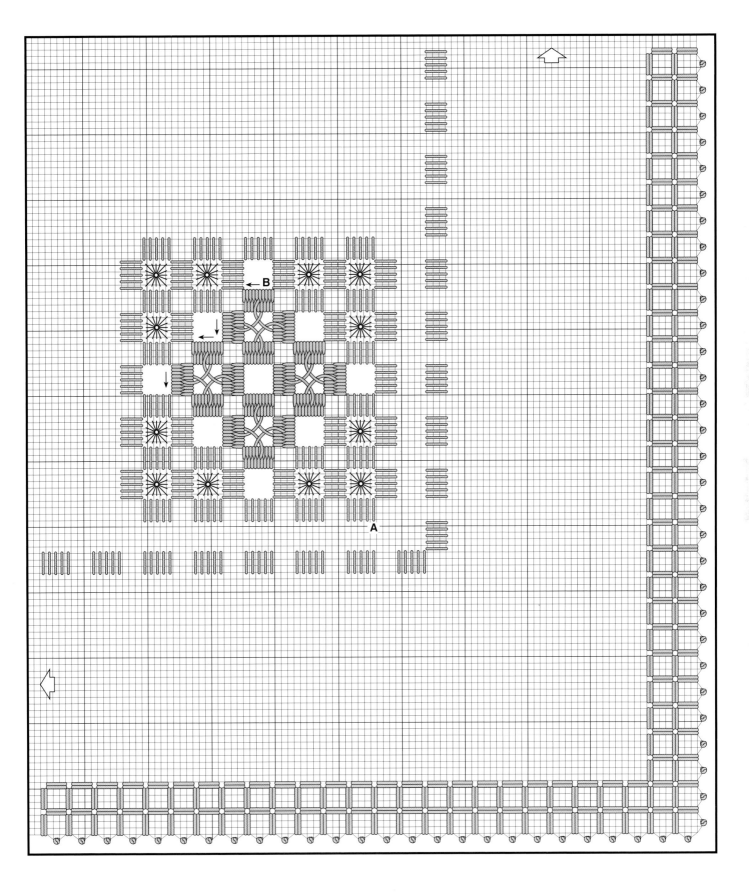

7 Looped picots, or square filets, could be added to the bars if you prefer.

8 Following all the instructions for completing a hem on page 30, mitre the corners and tack the hem line round the whole square, 40 threads from the outline of kloster blocks.

9 To stitch the double picot and open-sided square edging stitch, follow instructions on page 33. Use Coton Perlé No. 8 for the double picots and Coton Perlé No. 12 to secure the hem with open-sided square stitch. Trim the excess fabric.

10 Wash and press the work (see page 17).

KEY

	Stitch/Thread
	Kloster blocks DMC Coton Perlé No. 8
	Square eyelets DMC Coton Perlé No. 12
	Needleweaving with dove's eye DMC Coton Perlé No. 12
	Double picots with 2 rows of open-sided square stitch DMC Coton Perlé No. 12

CAFETIERE COVER

Keep the coffee warm by dressing up your cafetière in this jacket to give it a touch of elegance. The band of Hardanger and border stitches can be adapted to fit most sizes and colours could be chosen to match your china. A design of individual motifs incorporating eyelets and twisted bar filling is linked with reversed diagonal faggoting and kloster blocks. Bordered by a combination of twisted lattice band, kloster blocks and needleweaving, the bands form a decorative panel on the front and back of the cafetière. .

Finished size: 33 x 18 cm (13 x 7 in) to fit an 8-cup cafetière

Materials

Coffee coloured version
- 44.5 x 28 cm (17½ x 11 in) Jobelan evenweave, 28 threads to the inch, mid beige colour No. 07
- 1 ball of DMC Coton Perlé No. 8 No. 712
- 1 ball of DMC Coton Perlé No. 12 No. 712
- 1 ball of DMC Coton Perlé No. 12 No. 437 or Caron Collection Wildflower colour coral blush
- 45 x 30 cm (18 x 12 in) lining
- 35.5 x 20.5 cm (14 x 8 in) Polyfelt needled wadding
- 38 x 23 cm (15 x 9 in) coloured backing fabric for the embroidery
- 9 cm (3½ in) strip of Velcro
- Matching sewing thread

Antique White Version (Fabric and Threads)
- 44.5 x 28 cm (17½ x 11 in) Minster linen, 28 threads to the inch, antique white colour No. 402
- 1 ball of DMC Coton Perlé No. 8 No. 712
- 1 ball of DMC Coton Perlé No. 12 No. 712

Note: The design on the cafetière is easily adaptable to fit other sizes of coffee jug. If the jug is larger, compensate by adding extra space between the two design bands so that they become further apart. Add the same measurement to the ends – half on each side. If the jug is smaller, do the reverse. To adjust for the height, add on or take away motifs from the central panel to fit your requirements. The larger motif is 2.5 cm (1 in) high on 28 threads to the inch fabric, with the small kloster block square approximately 12 mm (½ in).

Method

1 Refer to the techniques section on pages 17–37. Prepare your fabric as described.

2 Following the chart and using white Coton Perlé No. 8, start the kloster blocks with your first stitch at A, 7 cm (2¾ in) up from the bottom edge and 14.2 cm (5⅝ in) in from the right-hand side edge.

3 Stitch all the central motifs separately and outline with the kloster block rectangle. Work the two straight lines of kloster blocks.

4 Complete the twisted lattice bands and satin stitch 'pyramids'.

5 Change to Coton Perlé No. 12 colour No. 437 to work the square eyelets and diagonal faggoting.

6 Cut and withdraw the threads between the straight lines of kloster blocks, a few inches at a time and needleweave with the Coton Perlé No. 12 colour No. 712.

7 Cut and withdraw the threads in the motifs needleweave starting at B and work twisted bars with picots if preferred.

8 To finish with a decorative hem, count 12 threads from the kloster blocks and work a back stitch with two rows of open-sided square edging stitch round the entire embroidery (see page 32), working to the measurements on the chart. Trim off the excess but leave a 12 mm (½ in) seam allowance.

9 Before making up, carefully wash and press the embroidery (see page 17).

10 Cut the backing and lining fabric to the size of the template, adding 12 mm (½ in) seam allowance.

11 Cut the wadding to the size of the template. Trim it all round to sit just inside the hem of the open square edging stitch. Place the trimmed wadding centrally on the wrong side of the backing fabric and stabilize with herringbone stitches lightly catching the outside edge.

12 Place the wadded backing fabric on to the lining fabric right sides together and machine close to the wadding leaving an opening between A and B (see template, page 126). Trim the excess fabric and turn inside out. Press if you want the cover to look less puffy.

13 To make the fastening tabs, cut two rectangles out of the remaining lining fabric or matching linen measuring 11.2 x 6 cm (4½ x 2½ in). Place right sides together and stitch three sides with a 12 mm (½ in) seam allowance, leaving open one longer side. Turn inside out, press and slip 12 mm (½ in) of the tab into the opening of the cover. Stitch up the opening securely.

14 Position the wadded piece of fabric on to the Hardanger embroidery, with the backing right side facing out, to sit just inside the edging stitch. Tack and slip stitch into place with small invisible stitches.

15 Cut the Velcro to fit the tab and stitch in place as shown on the template.

KEY

	Stitch/Thread
	Kloster blocks and satin stitch pyramids DMC Coton Perlé No. 8, Colour No. 712
	Twisted lattice band DMC Coton Perlé No. 8, Colour No. 712
	Satin stitch central motif DMC Coton Perlé No. 8, Colour No. 712
	Reversed diagonal faggoting DMC Coton Perlé No. 12, (Coffee-coloured version No. 437)
	Square eyelets DMC Coton Perlé No. 712, (Coffee-coloured version No. 437)
	Needleweaving DMC Coton Perlé No. 12, Colour No. 712
	Needleweaving with twisted bars (picots optional) DMC Coton Perlé No. 12, Colour 712
	Backstitch with open-sided square edging stitch DMC Coton Perlé No. 712, (Coffee-coloured version No. 437)

3.2 cm (1¼ in)

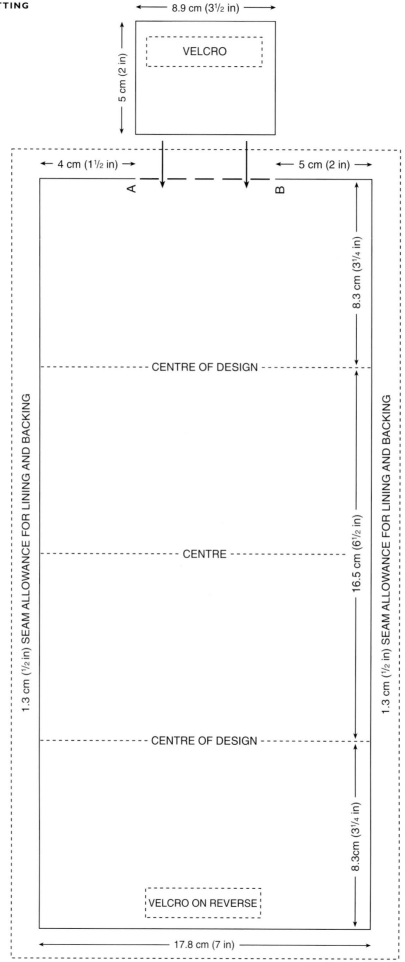

8.9 cm (3½ in)

VELCRO

5 cm (2 in)

4 cm (1½ in)

5 cm (2 in)

A

B

8.3 cm (3¼ in)

CENTRE OF DESIGN

1.3 cm (½ in) SEAM ALLOWANCE FOR LINING AND BACKING

CENTRE

16.5 cm (6½ in)

1.3 cm (½ in) SEAM ALLOWANCE FOR LINING AND BACKING

CENTRE OF DESIGN

8.3cm (3¼ in)

VELCRO ON REVERSE

17.8 cm (7 in)

NAPKIN RING

These delightfully simple napkin rings add the finishing touch to the perfect setting. With simple needleweaving and reversed diagonal faggoting, the design echoes the bread-basket cloth and table napkin so that they could be made as a set. Eyelets and the back stitch picot edging add to the decoration and they could be worked in any colour to match or contrast your table linen. Being simple and easy to complete means that it is not a major undertaking to make one napkin ring for each member of the family.

Finished size on 28 count linen: width 3.8 cm (1½ in), circumference 15 cm (6 in), diameter 3.8 cm (1½ in)

Materials
(for one table napkin ring)

White Version
- 15 x 26.5 cm (6 x 10½ in) Minster linen, 28 threads to the inch, colour white, or
- 18 x 28 cm (7 x 11 in) Zweigart Lugana, 25 threads to the inch, colour white
- 1 ball of DMC Coton Perlé No. 8 white
- 1 ball of DMC Coton Perlé No. 12 white

Blue and White Version
- 15 x 26.5 cm (6 x 10½ in) Minster linen, 28 threads to the inch, colour white
- 1 ball of DMC Coton Perlé No. 8 No. 797 Blue
- 1 ball of DMC Coton Perlé No. 12 white

Method

1 Refer to the techniques section on pages 17–37. Prepare your fabric as described and tack in the central vertical line.

2 Using the white Coton Perlé No. 8 and following the chart, begin working the kloster blocks. Start your first stitch at A, 5.5 cm (2¼ in) up from the edge of the fabric and two threads to the right of the vertical centre line .

3 Work the complete outline of kloster blocks and then fill in the blocks within the design.

4 Stitch the eyelets and reversed diagonal faggoting with the white Coton Perlé No. 12.

5 Cut and withdraw the threads of one section of the design and start needleweaving the bars at B following the directional arrows. Repeat in the other sections.

6 Knots or picots could be added to the bars if you wished (see blue and white version).

7 Before making up the napkin ring, wash and press the work (see page 17).

8 Join the seam across the width of the fabric, right sides together and matching up the pattern exactly.

9 On each side count up eight threads and pull out the ninth.

10 In this withdrawn line, work the first part of the back stitch picot edging (see page 32) using Coton Perlé No. 8. Fold over the edge to the inside and stitch one row of open-sided square stitch using Coton Perlé No. 12. Trim off the excess fabric close to the stitching.

KEY

Stitch/Thread

Kloster blocks
DMC Coton Perlé No. 8 (blue and white
version, Colour No. 797)

Reversed diagonal faggoting
DMC Coton Perlé No. 12 white

Square eyelets
DMC Coton Perlé No. 12 white

Needleweaving
DMC Coton Perlé No. 12 white

Back stitch picot with open-sided square stitch
DMC Coton Perlé No. 12 white

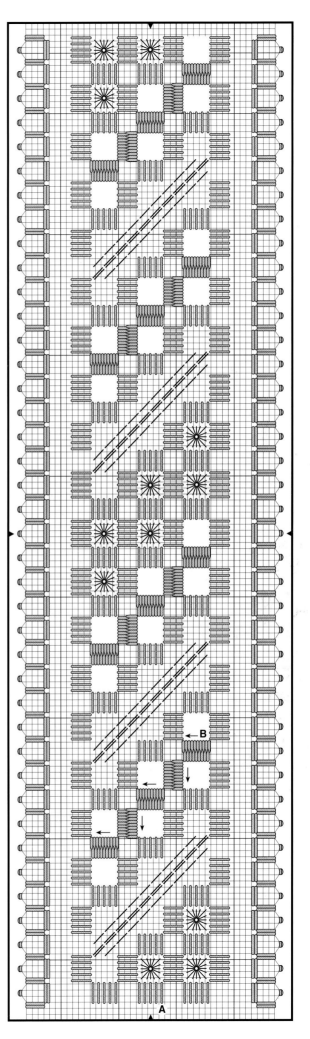

TABLE NAPKIN

Here is an invitation to eat. A starched white linen table napkin looks sophisticated and smart on any table. Fold it cleverly to show off the simple, delicate corner detail of open needlewoven corners with picot knots. Have fun and make coloured napkins to match contemporary opaque tableware or make a festive red set for Christmas.

Finished size: 40.5 cm (16 in) square

Materials
- 50 cm (19¾ in) square Minster linen, 28 threads to the inch, colour white
- 1 ball of DMC Coton Perlé No. 8 white
- 1 ball of DMC Coton Perlé No. 12 white

Note: The materials listed are for one table napkin. If you wish to change the dimensions of the napkin, refer to page 16 or if you decide to work a blue and white version, follow the directions, colourings and thickness of thread as described for the bread-basket cloth on page 114.

Method
1 Refer to the techniques section on pages 17–37. Prepare your fabric as described.

2 Lay the fabric flat in front of you and find the starting point A at the bottom right-hand corner, 7 cm (2¾ in) in from the lower edge of the fabric and 7.5 cm (3 in) in from the right-hand side edge.

3 Start your first kloster block at A using Coton Perlé No. 8 and work the outline triangle shape of the first corner. Fill in the rest of the design with the diagonal lines of kloster blocks as shown.

4 Continue stitching the line of kloster blocks from the corner of the design to link with the subsequent corner and work your way round back to the first corner. You will need 50 kloster blocks from corner to corner if you are using linen. It is best to complete

one corner of the design and let the rest of the design 'grow' from this first corner. (If you are having difficulty with the counting, refer to the instructions on page 16).

5 After completing the kloster blocks in all the corners, change your thread to the Coton Perlé No. 12 to work the reversed diagonal faggoting.

6 Only cut and withdraw the threads for needleweaving in the corner in which you are working. Begin the needleweaving at B, following the directional arrows on the chart. Complete each diagonal line of needleweaving before cutting and moving on to another (C), remembering to add the picots in the middle of each needlewoven square as shown.

7 Looped picots could be added to the bars if you prefer.

8 To make up the hem follow all instructions for completing a hem on page 30 and mitre the corners. Tack the hem 12 threads from the outline of kloster blocks round the whole square (pin stitch hemming will be worked in this line).

9 Count eight threads for the actual hem turnings, with an inside turning of seven threads. As the fabric will fray, only work on one side at a time.

10 Use Coton Perlé No. 12 white to secure the hem with pin stitch (see page 32).

11 Wash and press the work (see page 17).

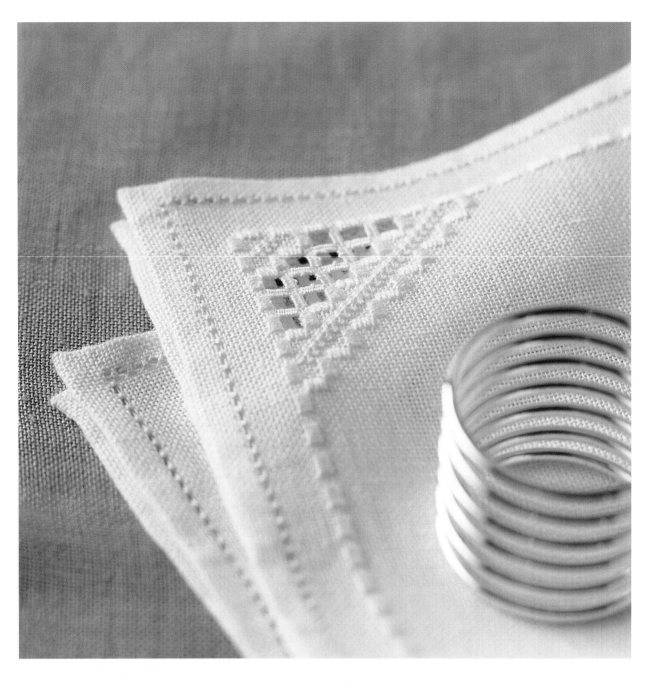

KEY

Stitch/Thread

Kloster blocks
DMC Coton Perlé No. 8

Reversed diagonal faggoting
DMC Coton Perlé No. 12 white

Needleweaving with looped picots
DMC Coton Perlé No. 12 white

Pin stitch hem
DMC Coton Perlé No. 12 white

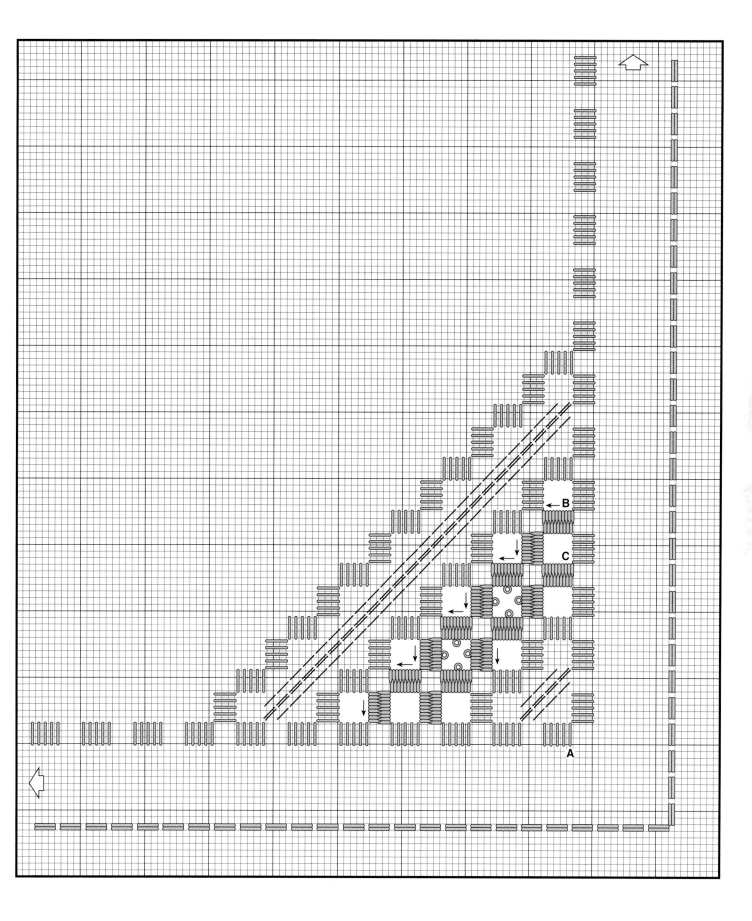

TABLECLOTH

A traditional fresh white tablecloth sets the scene for any occasion – a romantic dinner, special festive occasions – or just to impress. The tessellated design of crosses, linked with a diamond shape surrounding the satin stitch motif, runs down the middle of the tablecloth. Eyelets and a filling of square filets create the delicate open effect.

Finished size: to fit your own table
Finished size of central design: 40.5 x 12.5 cm (16 x 5 in)
Design repeat : 14.5 cm (5¾ in) or 160 threads

Materials
• Use measurements to fit your own table Minster linen, 28 threads to the inch, colour white
• 1 ball of DMC Coton Perlé No. 8 white
• 1 ball of DMC Coton Perlé No. 12 white

Method
1 Refer to the techniques section on pages 17–37. Prepare your fabric as described and tack in the central vertical and horizontal lines.

2 Start your first kloster block at A using Coton Perlé No. 8, 22 threads down from the centre point and two threads to the right of the central vertical line.

3 Complete the small diamond shape and, following the chart, methodically work outwards stitching the design outline of kloster blocks with as many repeats as you need and fill in the central 'ship' motif.

4 Changing your thread to Coton Perlé No. 12, complete all the diagonal and square eyelets, followed by the reversed diagonal faggoting.

5 Cut and withdraw the threads for needleweaving as shown on the chart and fill in with square filets starting at B following the directional arrows, and include picot knots if you prefer (see dressing-table mat step 10, page 112). Alternative fillings may be used.

6 To make up the hem, follow all instructions for completing a hem on page 30 and mitre the corners.

7 Depending on the size of your tablecloth, make hem turnings between 12 and 20 threads wide with an inside turning of one less thread.

8 Use Coton Perlé No. 12 to secure the hem with pin stitch (see page 32). If you want to have a more decorative border to the hem edge, work a ladder hem stitch (see page 31).

9 Wash and press the work (see page 17).

Note: The tessellated design of linked motifs for the tablecloth is not only simple to understand but is extremely versatile and adaptable.

Adapting the size
• To increase the area of stitching add more repeats, either lengthways or widthways or both.
• The design may be converted to form a square border inset. Use the 'cross' shape motif for the corner turning and develop the rest of the design from either side of this shape. Add as many repeats as are necessary to meet your measurements.
• For a runner, outline the finished design with buttonhole stitch edging and cut away from the background.
• To add another dimension, frame and echo the completed design with a further outline of kloster blocks (twelve threads away) leaving space to work reversed diagonal faggoting between the two lines of kloster blocks.

KEY

Stitch/Thread

||||||
Kloster blocks
DMC Coton Perlé No. 8

Ship motifs
DMC Coton Perlé No. 8

Square eyelets
DMC Coton Perlé No. 12

Diagonal eyelets
DMC Coton Perlé No. 12

Reversed diagonal faggoting
DMC Coton Perlé No. 12

Needleweaving with square filets
DMC Coton Perlé No. 12

Pin stitched hem
DMC Coton Perlé No. 12

Needleweaving with picot knots
DMC Coton Perlé No. 12

LIST OF SUPPLIERS

UNITED KINGDOM

DMC Creative World plc
Pullman Road
Wigston
Leicester LE8 2DY
Tel: 0116 281 1040
Fax: 0116 281 3592
Suppliers of all embroidery needs,
threads, linen, etc. Telephone for the
nearest stockist.

Fabric Flair Ltd
Northlands Industrial Estate
Copheap Lane
Warminster
Wiltshire BA12 OBG
Freefone: 0800 716851
Tel: 01985 846400
Fax: 01985 846849
Suppliers of linen and cotton
fabrics. Telephone for the nearest
stockist.

Coats Crafts UK
PO Box 22
The Lingfield Estate
Mc Mullen Road
Darlington
Co Durham DL1 1YQ

Consumer Services Helpline:
01325 365 457
Suppliers of all embroidery needs,
Anchor threads, linen, etc.
Telephone or write for the nearest
stockist.

Household Articles Ltd
Sanderstead Station approach
South Croydon
Surrey CR2 OYY
Tel: 0181 651 6321
Fax: 0181 651 4095
For suppliers of La Cafetière.
Telephone for the nearest stockist.

Macleod Craft Marketing
West Yonderton
Warlock Road
Bridge of Weir
Renfrewshire PA11 3SR
Tel/fax : 01505 612618
The Caron Collection of variegated
hand-dyed threads. Telephone for
the nearest stockist.

Oliver Twists
34 Holmlands Park
Chester Le Street
County Durham DH3 3PJ
Tel/fax : 0191 388 8233
Hand-dyed threads, fabrics and fibres.

Janome UK Ltd
Janome Centre
Southside
Bredbury
Stockport
Cheshire SK6 2SP
Tel: 0161 666 6011
Range of scissors. Telephone for the
nearest stockist.

Ribbon Designs
42 Lake View
Edgware
Middlesex HA8 7RU
Tel: 0181 958 4966
Mail-order service for ribbons,
including full range of pure silk
ribbons and ribbons for embroidery.

The Bead Merchant
38 Eld Lane
Colchester
Essex CO1 1LS
Tel: 01206 764101
Fax: 01206 764202
All beads and bead supplies
(including Delica beads).
Mail order service.

Shades at Mace and Nairn
89 Crane Street
Salisbury
Wiltshire SP1 2PY
Tel: 01722 336903
Embroidery specialists, supplying
everything for the embroiderer.

Malmesbury Silks
2 Old Rectory Cottage
Easton Grey
Malmesbury
Wiltshire SN16 OPE
Tel: 01666 840881
Myriad selection of silk threads.

John Lewis Partnership
Oxford Street
London W1A 1EX
Tel: 0171 629 7711
Extensive haberdashery department,
including selection of cushion pads.

The Bead Shop
21a Tower Street
Covent Garden
London WC2H 9NS

UNITED STATES

**Anchor Threads Coats &
Clark/Susan Bates**
30 Patewood Dr. Ste. 351
Greenville SC 29615
1-864-234-0331
www.coatsandclark.com

Charles Crafts, Inc.
PO Box 1049
Laurinburg, NC 28353
Consumer Line
1-800-277-0980
www.charlescraft.com

Daniel Enterprises
306 McKay St.
Laurinburg, NC 28352
1-910-277-7441
1-800-277-6850
www.crafterspride.com

Lee's Needlearts, Inc.
5630 East Route 38
Pennsauken, NJ 08109
1-609-665-8323

Norden Crafts
502 Morse Avenue, Unit K
Schaumberg, IL 60193
Tel: 1-847-891-0770
Fax: 1-847-891-0976

Nordic Needle
1314 Gateway Dr. SW
Fargo, ND 58103
1-701-235-5231
1-800-433-4321
www.nordicneedle.com

Sudberry House
12 Colton Road
PO Box 895
Old Lyme, CT 06371
www.Connix. Com/~Sudberry/

The DMC Corporation
10 Port Kearny
South Kearny, NJ 07032
1-973-589-0606
www.DMC-USA.com

Zweigart/Joan Toggit, Ltd.
2 Riverview Drive
Somerset, NJ 08873-1139
1-732-271-1943
www.Zweigart.com

NORWAY

Håndarbeidshuset A/S
Skovveien 29
0257 Oslo
Norway
Tel: (00 47) 22 44 18 10
Fax: (00 47) 22 44 95 54
Suppliers of fabric and thread for
Hardanger embroidery, DMC,
books etc.

Husfliden A/S
Møllergata 4
0181 Oslo,
Norway
Tel: (00 47) 22 42 10 75
Fax: (00 47) 22 42 12 24

Suppliers of fabric and thread for
Hardanger embroidery, designs and
materials for making a bunad,
DMC, books, etc

Heimen Husflid
Rosenkrantz Gate 8
0159 Oslo
Norway
Tel: (00 47) 22 41 40 50
Fax: (00 47) 22 42 03 40
Suppliers of fabric and thread for
Hardanger embroidery, designs and
materials for making a bunad,
DMC, books, etc

Bunadsbua ANS
Rykkje 7
5610 Nordheimsund
Norway
Tel: (00 47) 56 55 55 26
Suppliers of designs and materials
for the traditional bunad

Husfliden A/S
Vågsallm. 3
5014 Bergen
Tel: (00 47) 55 31 78 70
Suppliers of fabric and thread for
Hardanger embroidery, designs and
materials for making a bunad,

ACKNOWLEDGEMENTS

Wonderful friends and students have generously given their time and expertise in working extra samples and projects for this book. I give special thanks to Sarah Nichols, Jane Corin, Kate Haslam, Lynne Fox, Barbara Slade, Lynda Gould, Ann Carter, Tina Holland, Gillian Bray, Moya Jolley and Penny Evans Jones for all their skill, interest and enthusiasm, which have played an integral part in creating this book. Thanks also for the talents and help of Jan Sugden and Ruby Lever in making up some of the projects, and for the encouragement, behind the scenes, of Ann Bartleet.

I thank my friends in Norway, who have patiently and generously shared their own knowledge of Hardanger with me and who have helped me with the Norwegian names for stitches: Ågot Gammersvik, Director of the Hardanger Folkemuseum, Utne; Kari-Anne Pederson, Assistant Curator for textiles and dress at the Norsk Folkemuseum, Oslo; and Margherita Ficko, Conservation Technician at the Norsk

Folkemuseum, Oslo.

Thank you to my editors, Venetia Penfold, Emma Clegg and Christopher Fagg and DWN's designer, Vicky Harvey, for their encouragement and hard work while producing my book. Much recognition and appreciation go to my illustrator, Siriol Clarry, for her meticulous diagrams and charts, and to Janine Hosegood and Michael Wicks for their stunning photographs.

I gratefully acknowledge the generous contributions of materials, fabrics and equipment from Cara Ackerman of DMC Creative World, Malcolm Turner of Fabric Flair, Alistair McMinn of Coats Craft UK, David Macleod of Macleod Craft Marketing, Valerie Fay of Household Articles Ltd, Maureen Brown of Janome UK Ltd, Marilyn Becker of Ribbon Designs, Jean Oliver of Oliver Twists, Hilary Williams of The Silk Route, and Jill Devon of The Bead Merchant.

INDEX